AF082798

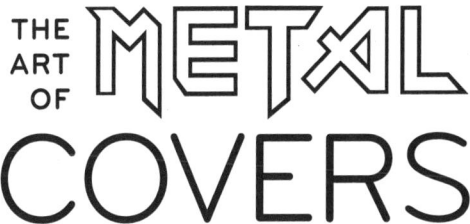

THE ART OF METAL COVERS

VOLUME 02

"I believe every guitar player inherently has something unique about their playing. They just have to identify what makes them different and develop it."

**Jimmy Page, Led Zeppelin**

## Has metal lost its shock factor?

The artworks, though meant to be provocative and shocking, are today a part of popular culture. All of a sudden, designs from Iron Maiden, Kiss, and Motörhead album covers can be found at discount or fabric stores – or perhaps this is exactly the point?

Monsters, skulls, and pentagrams simply hold a certain fascination for people who don't listen to metal. This has since helped Eddie, Snaggletooth, Knarrenheinz or Vic Rattlehead become nearly as popular as the bands featuring them on their album covers. Other designs have also taken on legendary status, such as Vince Locke's bloodthirsty drawings for Cannibal Corpse, Axel Hermann's sinister illustrations for bands like Unleashed, Asphyx, and Iced Earth, or John Dyer Baizley's mix of art nouveau and baroque adorning the covers for his own band (Baroness).

The band photo is also an art form that is celebrated in metal like no other genre. This includes oiled up men in fur trousers, a lonely black metaller captured wearing corpse paint, or the nicest of people adopting a particularly grim pose for the camera. The cover design is rounded off with the band logo. The font alone lets you know whether you've got your hands on a black, death, or thrash metal album. Very few band logos outside the genre are so easily recognisable.

Everything is allowed... well almost! With such as diverse range of designs, no other genre has had so much trouble with censorship. While sometimes justified (the original album for Scorpions' Virgin Killer being a case in point), this comes across as excessive in many instances. Metal still needs to give you a bit of a shock, right?

**Christian Kind**
Vinyl metal collector and owner of
the record store "Plattenkiste", Hamburg, 2022

# SCAN THE SPOTIFY CODES TO PLAY EVERY ALBUM INSTANTLY! *

**1.**
Click the search bar in your **Spotify** app.
Then tip the camera 📷 icon at the top right.

**2.**
Scan the printed **Spotify**
code on the calendar page.

**3.**
Enjoy the music!

*\* Please note: Not all bands present themselves on Spotify,
so there are various albums without a code.*

**Praying Mantis**
**Time Tells No Lies**
Arista, 1981
Rodney Matthews (Design)

01 JAN

**Megadeth**
**Peace Sells... But Who's Buying**
Capitol Records, 1986
Andy Somers, Dave Mustaine (Design)
Edward J. Repka (Illustration)

02 JAN

**Coven**
**Blood On The Snow**
Buddah Records, 1974
Milton Sincoff (Design)
Ann Miller (Illustration)

03 JAN

**Church Of Misery**
**Master Of Brutality**
Rise Above Records, 2011
Cover Artists Unknown

04 JAN

**Motörhead**
**Bomber**
Bronze, 1979
Curtis Evans (Design)

05  JAN

**Scorpions**
**Fly To The Rainbow**
RCA Victor, 1974
Petrus Wandrey (Design)

06 JAN

**Pestilence**
**Spheres**
Roadrunner Records, 1993
Dan Seagrave (Illustration)

07 JAN

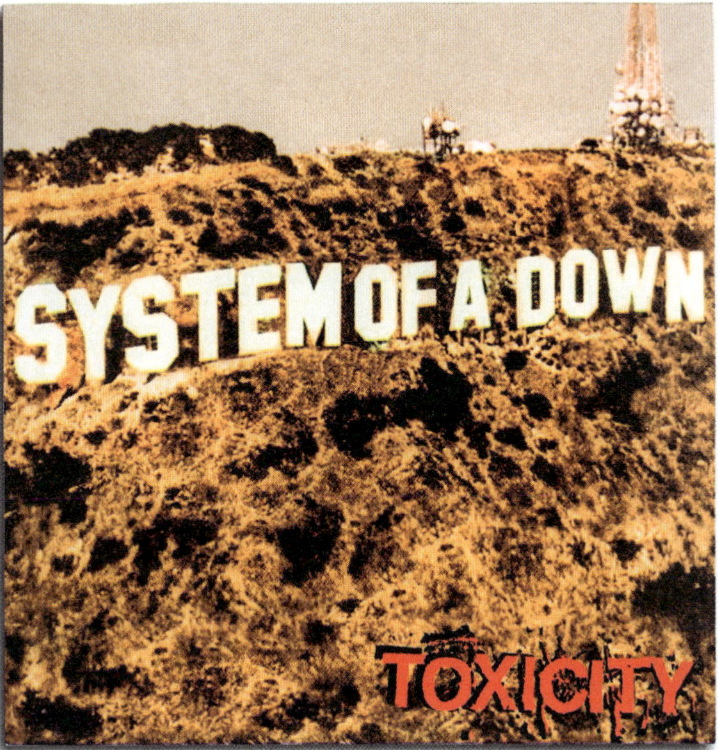

**System Of A Down**
**Toxicity**
American Recordings, 2001
System Of A Down (Design)
Mark Wakefield (Photo)

# 08 JAN

# Get the most exclusive, handmade oak stand for your vinyl calendar.

**www.seltmannpublishers.com**
Worldwide shipping, free within Germany

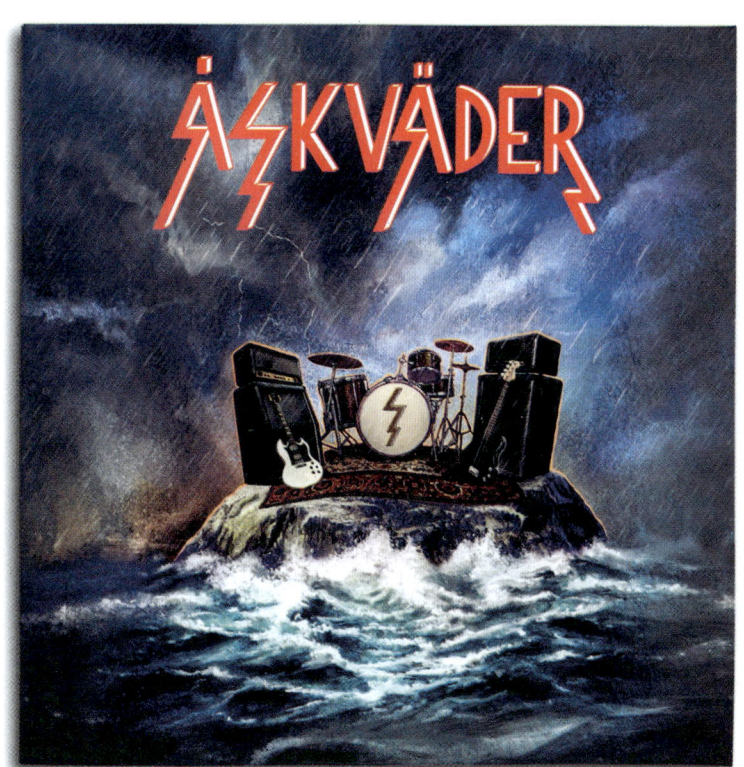

**Åskväder**
The Sign Records, 2020
Isabelle Gut, Johan Leion (Design)

09 JAN

**Vladimir Harkonnen**
**Into Dreadnought Fever**
Obey! Records, 2014
Jochen "Fritte" Möning (Illustration)

# 10 JAN

**Black Sabbath**
**Sabbath Bloody Sabbath**
WWA Records, 1973
Pacific Eye & Ear (Design)
Drew Struzman (Photo)

# 11 JAN

**The Riven**
The Sign Records, 2019
Maarten Sonders (Illustration)

12 JAN

**Unleashed**
**Across The Open Sea**
Century Media, 1993
Axel Hermann (Illustration)

13 JAN

**Kvelertak**
**Nattesferd**
Indie Recordings, 2016
Deformat (Design)
Arik Rooper (Illustration)

**14** JAN

**The Gun**
**Gun**
CBS, 1968
W. Roger Dean (Design)

15 JAN

**Toxic Holocaust**
**Conjure And Command**
Relapse Records, 2011
Dave Schiff, Joel Grind (Design)
Danile "Sawblade" Shaw (Illustration)

# 16 JAN

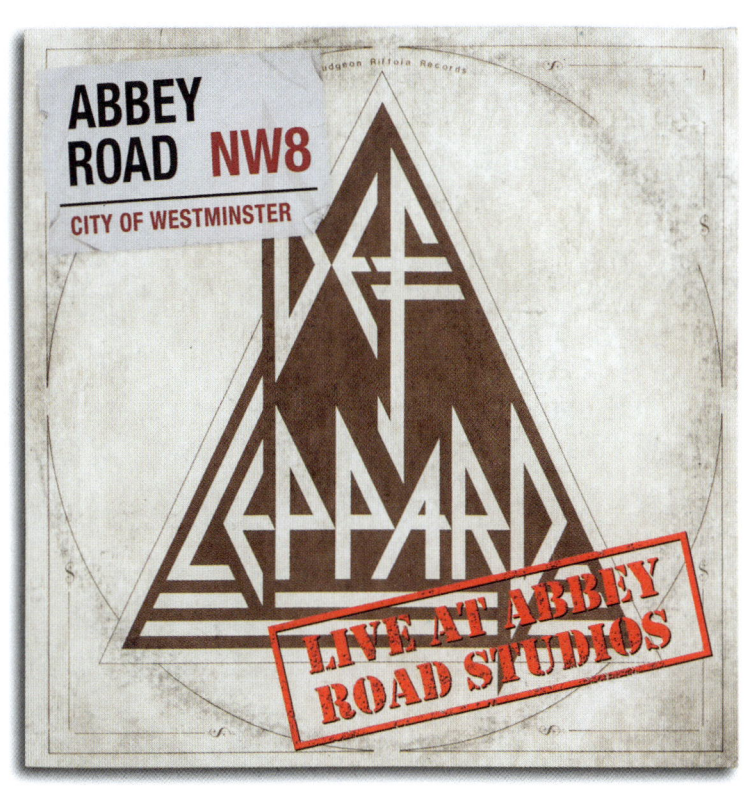

**Def Leppard**
**Live At Abbey Road Studios**
UMC, 2018
Cover Artists Unknown

# 17 JAN

**The Neptune Power Federation**
**Music From Lucifer's Universe**
Cruz del Sur Music, 2019
Mike Foxall (Design)

# 18 JAN

**Suicidal Tendencies**
Frontier Records, 1983
Dee Zee (Design)
Glen E. Friedman (Photo)

# 19 JAN

**High Spirits**
**Another Night**
High Roller Records, 2011
Scott Hoffman (Design)

**20** JAN

**Devil's Day Off**
**Stop The Clock**
JanML Records, 2020
Claudia von Bihl (Design)

## 21 JAN

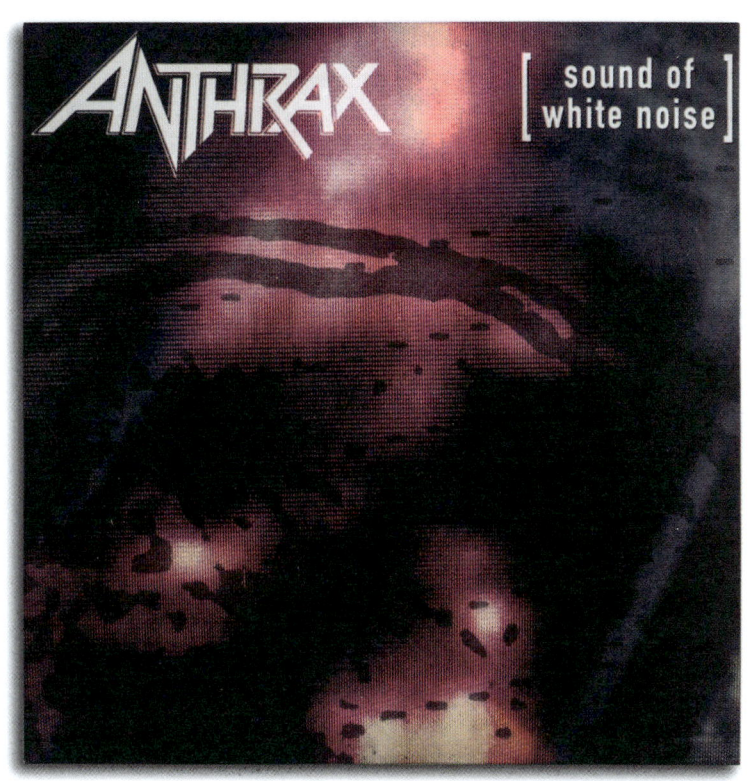

**Anthrax**
**Sound Of White Noise**
Elektra, 1993
Robyn Lynch (Design)
Charlie Benante, Paul Elledge (Photo)

22 JAN

**King Buffalo**
**Dead Star**
King Buffalo Self Released, 2020
Scott Donaldson (Design)
Ryan T. Hancock (Illustration)

23 JAN

**Death**
**Leprosy**
Combat, 1998
David Bett (Design)
Edward J. Repka (Illustration)

24 JAN

**Grand Magus**
**Hammer Of The North**
Roadrunner Records, 2010
Necrolord (Design)

# 25 JAN

**Savatage**
**Edge Of Thorns**
Atlantic, 1993
Gary Smith (Design)

# 26 JAN

**Khemmis**
**Doomed Heavy Metal**
20 Buick Spin, 2020
Cameron Hinojosa (Illustration)

## 27 JAN

**Detraktor**
**Grinder**
Violent Creek Records, 2019
Heiko Kramer (Illustration)

28 JAN

**Slayer**
**Seasons In The Abyss**
Def American Recordings, 1990
Robert Fisher (Design)
Larry Carroll (Illustration)

## 29 JAN

**Judas Priest**
**Screaming For Vengeance**
CBS, 1982
John Berg (Design)
Doug Johnson (Illustration)

30 JAN

**Alice Cooper**
**Love It To Death**
Warner Bros. Records, 2010
Prigent (Photo)

31 JAN

**Mammoth Mammoth**
**Kreuzung**
Napalm Records, 2019
Mammoth Mammoth (Design)

01 FEB

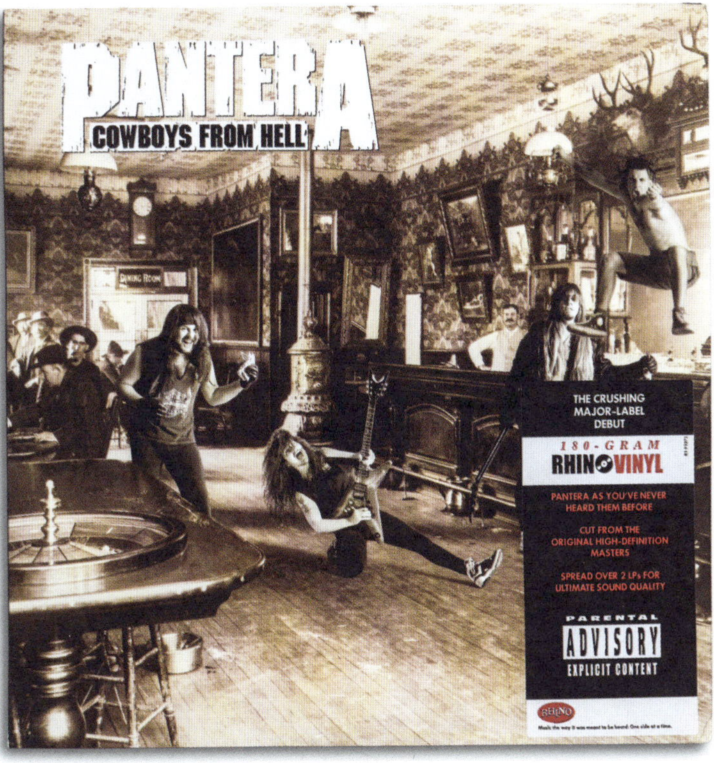

**Pantera**
**Cowboys From Hell**
ATCO Records, 1990
Bob Defrin (Design)
Bettman Archive (Photo)

02 FEB

**Inter Arma**
**Garbers Days Revisited**
Relapse Records, 2020
Brian Mercer (Design)

03 FEB

**Warlock**
**Triumph And Agony**
Vertigo, 1987
Geoffrey Gillespie (Illustration)

04 FEB

**Emissary Of Suffering
Mournful Sights**
Cold Knife Records, 2021
Matthias Settele (Design)
Evelyn Steinweg (Illustration)

05 FEB

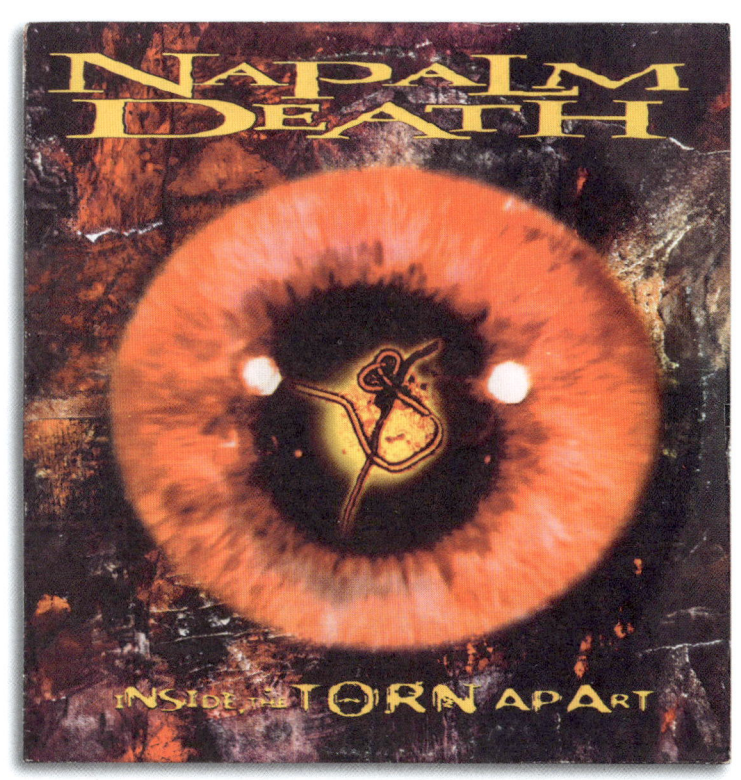

**Napalm Death**
**Inside The Torn Apart**
Earache, 1997
Graham Humpreys (Design)

06 FEB

**Deep Purple**
**Fireball**
Harvest, 1971
Castle, Chappell & Partners Limited (Design)
Tony Burrett (Photo)

## 07 FEB

**Audrey Horne**
**Blackout**
Napalm Records, 2018
Asle Birkeland (Design)
Bent Rene Synnevåg (Photo)

08 FEB

**Mayhem**
**De Mysteriis Dom. Sathanas**
Deathlike Silence Productions, 2020
DYE (Design)
Lasse A. Scherven (Illustration)

## 09 FEB

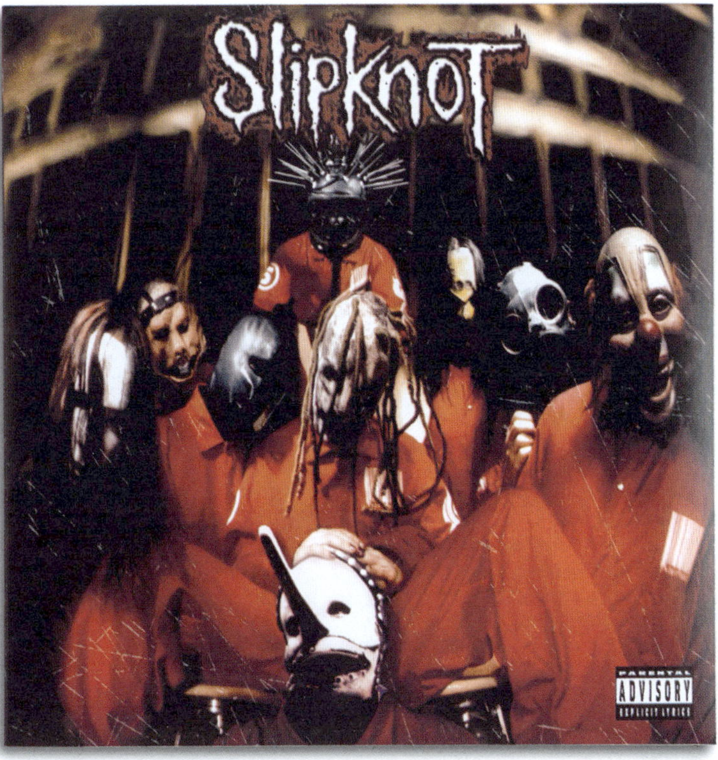

**Slipknot**
Roadrunner Records, 1999
Slipknot (Design)
Stefan Seskis (Photo)

10 FEB

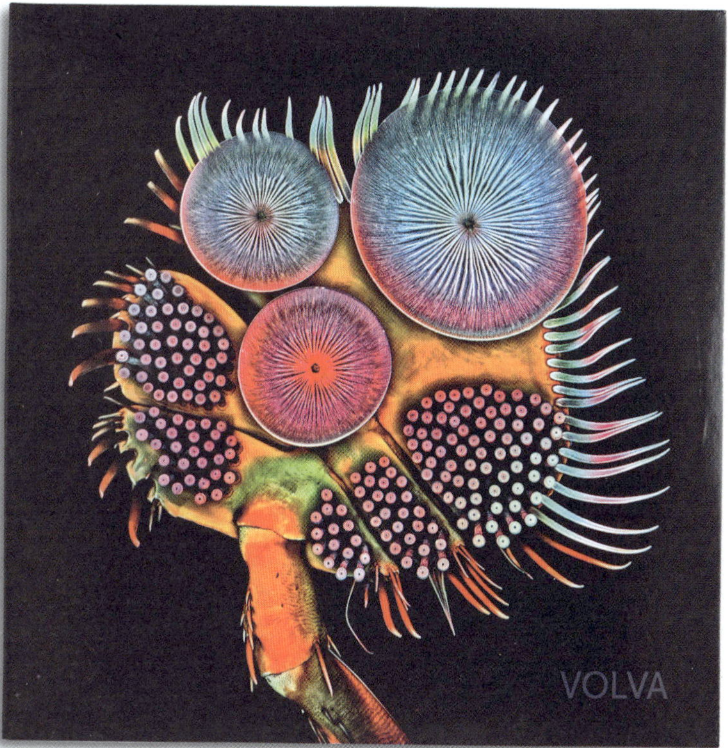

**Echolot**
**Volva**
Czar of Crickets, 2017
Luca Piattalonga (Design)
Igor Siwanowicz (Illustration)

**11** FEB

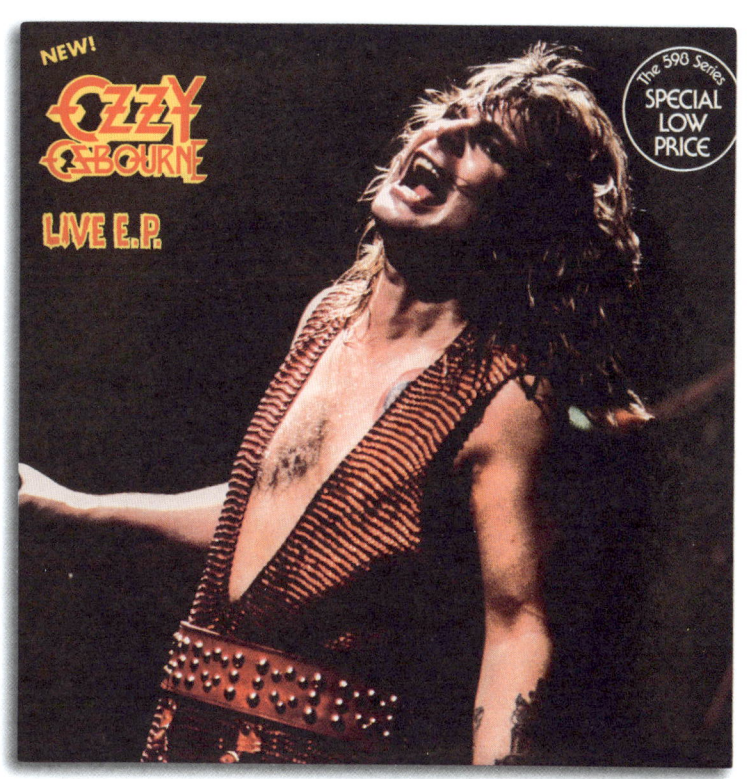

**Ozzy Osbourne**
**Live E.P.**
Jet Records, 1982
Art Graham (Design)
Robert Ellis (Photo)

# 12 FEB

**Riot**
**Fire Down Under**
Elektra Records, 1981
Marcia Loeb (Design)
Steve Weiss (Illustration)

# 13 FEB

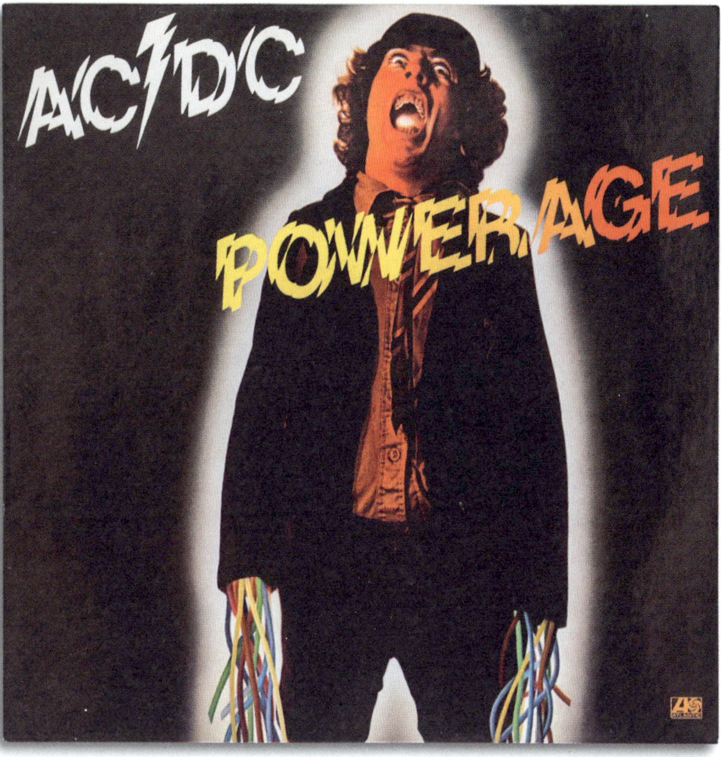

**AC/DC**
Powerage
Albert Productions, 1978
Bob Defrin (Design)
Jim Houghton (Photo)

14 FEB

**Spirit Adrift**
**Enlightened In Eternity**
Century Media, 2020
Adam Burke (Design)

15 FEB

**Benediction**
**Subconscious Terror**
Nuclear Blast, 1990
Cover Artists Unknown

16 FEB

**Crypt Sermon**
**The Ruins Of Fading Light**
Dark Descent Records, 2019
Mark Wohlberg (Design)
Brooks Wilson (Illustration)

17 FEB

**Hatriot**
**Heroes Of Origin**
Massacre Records, 2013
Cover Artists Unknown

18 FEB

**Saxon**
**Denim And Leather**
Carrere, 1981
Cover Artists Unknown

19 FEB

**Godslave**
**In Hell**
Day One Records, 2013
Cover Artists Unknown

20 FEB

**Pentagram**
**Relentless**
Peaceville, 1993
Cover Artists Unknown

21 FEB

**Helix**
**White Lace & Black Leather**
H&S Records, 1981
Cover Artists Unknown

## 22 FEB

**At The Gates**
**Purgatory Unleashed – Live At Wacken**
Earache, 2010
Cover Artists Unknown

23 FEB

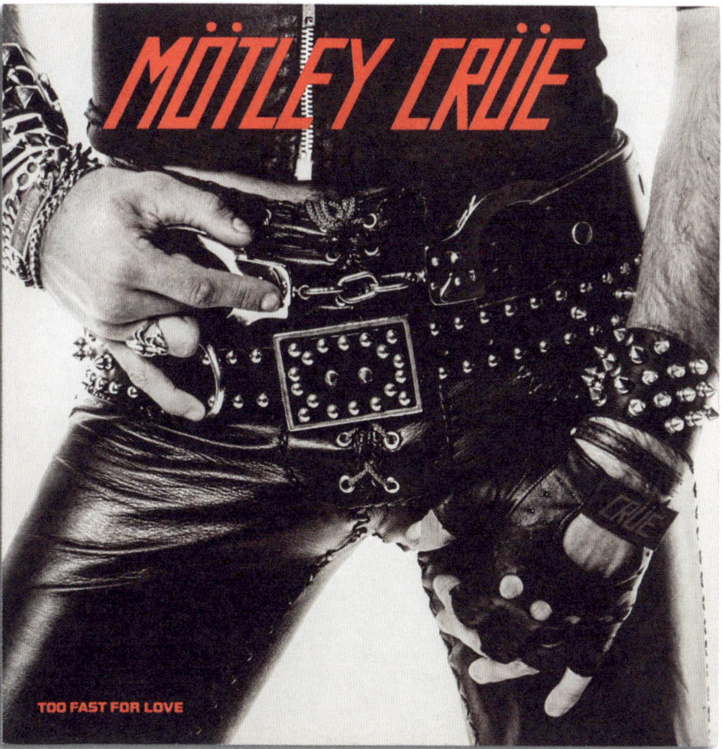

**Mötley Crue**
**Too Fast For Love**
Leathür Records, 1981
Coffman & Coffman Productions (Design)
Debra Meyer, Michael Pinter (Photo)

24 FEB

**Lightsabres**
**A Shortcut To Insanity**
DHU Records, 2018
John Strömshed, Midori Hayashi, Shane Horror (Design)
Midori Hayashi (Photo)

## 25 FEB

S.O.D.: **Stormtroopers Of Death**
**Speak English Or Die**
Roadrunner Records, 1985
Charlie Benante (Design)

26 FEB

**Unleashed**
**Across The Open Sea**
Century Media, 1993
Axel Hermann (Design)

27 FEB

**Hypocrisy**
**Worship**
Nuclear Blast, 2021
Marcelo Vasco (Design)
Blake Armstrong (Illustration)

28 FEB

**Various Artists**
**Brutal Africa – The Heavy Metal Cowboys Of Botswana**
Svart Records, 2019
Ville Valavuo (Design)
Pep Bonet (Photo)

# 29 FEB

**Ophidian I**
**Desolate**
Season of Mist, 2021
Cover Artists Unknown

# 01 MAR

**Iron Maiden**
**Somewhere In Time**
EMI, 1986
Derck Riggs, Rod Smallwood (Design)
Derek ‚Master Of The Universe' Riggs (Illustration)

## 02  MAR

**Fear Factory**
**Genexus**
Nuclear Blast Entertainment, 2015
Anthony Clakrson (Design)

03 MAR

**Queen**
**Live At The Rainbow '74**
Hollywood Records, 2014
Richard Gray (Design)

# 04 MAR

**The Obsessed**
**The Church Within**
Real Gone Music, 2013
The Obsessed (Design)
David Foye (Illustration)

05 MAR

**Biohazard**
**State Of The World Address**
Warner Bros. Records, 1994
Kim Champagne (Design)
Ken Schles, Mike Hashimoto, Paul D'Amato (Photo)

06 MAR

**Heretic**
**Alive Under Satan**
Ván, 2015
Tony Hellfire (Design)
Karmazid (Illustration)

07 MAR

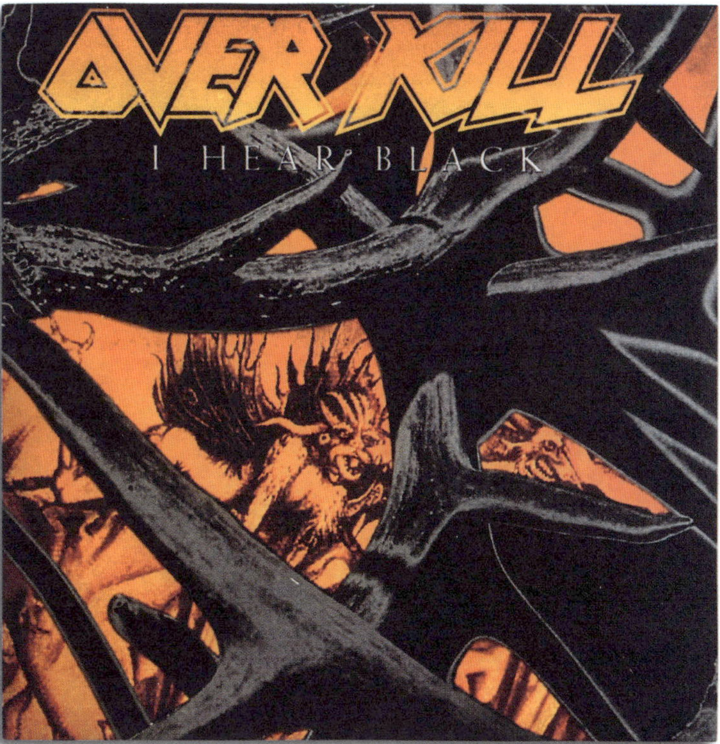

**Overkill**
**I Hear Black**
Atlantic, 1993
Mikel (Illustration)

08 MAR

**The Black Wizards**
**What The Fuzz!**
Ragingplanet, 2017
João Maio Pinto (Design)

09 MAR

**Napalm Death**
**Harmony Corruption**
Earache, 1990
David Windmill (Design)

10 MAR

**Anvil**
**Legal At Last**
AFM Records, 2020
W. "Cliff" Knese (Design)

11 MAR

**Wo Fat**
**Midnight Cometh**
Ripple Music, 2016
David Paul Seymour (Illustration)

12 MAR

**Dew-Scented**
**Incinerate**
Bastarized Recordings, 2007
Killustrations (Design)

# 13 MAR

**Black Sabbath**
**Feels Good To Me**
I.R.S. Records, 1990
Cover Artists Unknown

# 14 MAR

**Motörhead**
**1916**
Epic, 1991
Craig Nelson (Design)

15 MAR

**Sijjin**
**Angel Of The Eastern Gate**
Sephulchral Voice, 2020
Theby (Design)
Timn (Illustration)

16 MAR

**Triptykon**
**Melana Chasmata**
Century Media, 2014
Marsen Angler, Tom Gabriel Warrior (Design)
H.R. Giger (Illustration)

# 17 MAR

**Final Cry**
**The Ever-Rest**
MDD Records, 2021
Kai Wilhelm (Design)
Mateusz Latocha, Samuraj Design (Illustration)

**Black Trip**
**Shadowline**
Threeman Recordings, 2015
Kristofer Ekeblom (Design)

# 19 MAR

**Darkened**
**Kingdom Of Decay**
Edged Circle Productions, 2020
Cover Artists Unknown

20 MAR

**Admiral Sir Cloudeley Shovell**
**Check Em Before You Wreck Em**
Rise Above Records, 2014
Andy Morten (Design)
Esther Segarra (Photo)

21 MAR

**Celtic Frost**
**To Mega Therion**
Sanctuary Records, 1985
Tom Gabriel Warrior (Design)
H.R. Giger (Illustration)

22 MAR

**Shok Paris**
**Full Metal Jacket**
No Remorse Records, 2020
Alex Yarborough (Design)
Jan Bünnig (Photo)

23 MAR

**Warpig**
Fonthill, 1972
Cover Artists Unknown

24 MAR

**Inglorious**
**We Will Ride**
Frontiers Music SRL, 2021
Paul Tippett (Design)

25 MAR

**Pentagram**
Esen Müzik, 2021
Faruk Acar (Design)
Tunç Örer (Illustration)

26 MAR

**Saxon**
**Denim And Leather**
Carrere, 1981
Cover Artists Unknown

# 27 MAR

**Pestilence**
**Ex|T|Vm**
Agonia Records, 2021
Michał "Xaay Loran" (Illustration)

# 28 MAR

**Year Of The Cobra**
**Burn Your Dead**
Magnetic Eye Records, 2017
Joshua M. Wilkinson (Design)

29 MAR

**Destruction**
**Under Attack**
Nuclear Blast, 2016
Gyula Havancsak (Design)

30 MAR

**Necrophobic**
**Bloodhymns**
Hammerheart Records, 2002
Claes Berkes (Design)

# 31   MAR

**Traitor**
**Venomizer**
Violent Creek Records, 2015
Andrei Bouzikov (Design)

01 APR

**Screamer**
**Adrenaline Distractions**
High Roller Records, 2011
Cover Artists Unknown

02 APR

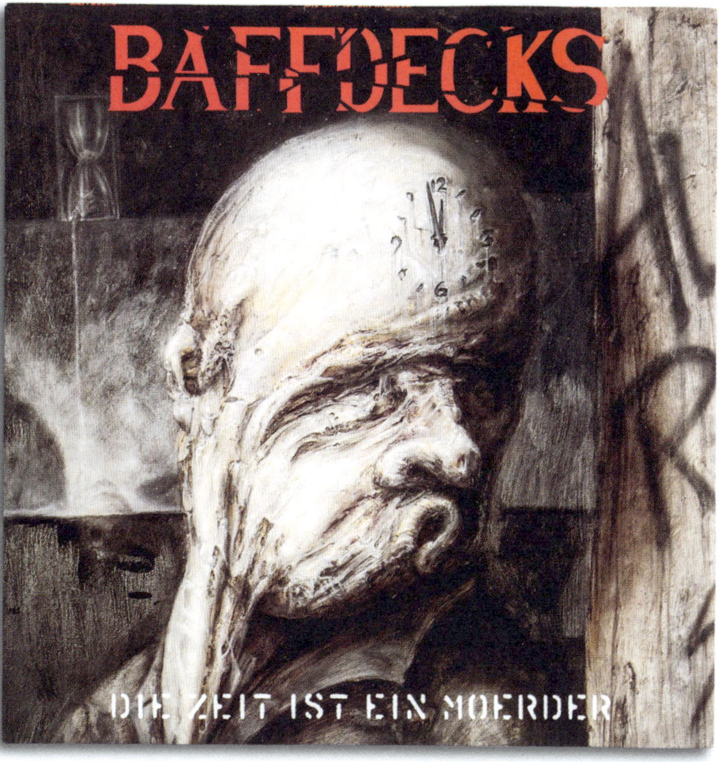

**Baffdecks**
**Die Zeit ist ein Moerder**
Armageddon, 1993
Medici Photodesign (Design)
Atelier A. Hella (Illustration)

03 APR

**Ghost**
**Popestar**
Loma Vista, 2016
Mikael Eriksson (Design)
Necropolitus Cracoviensis Zbigniew Bielak (Illustration)

04 APR

**Power From Hell**
**Blood'N'Spikes**
Dying Victims Productions, 2018
Welling Ramos (Design)

## 05 APR

**Karnivool**
**Asymetry**
Cymatic Records, 2015
Debaser (Design)
Rene Almanza (Illustration)

06 APR

**High Spirits**
**Motivator**
High Roller Records, 2016
Alex von Wieding (Design)
Alex von Wieding (Illustration)

07 APR

**Paragon**
**Controlled Demolition**
Massacre Records, 2019
Aldo Requena, Jan Bünning (Design)
Aldo "V" Requena (Illustration)

08 APR

**Uriah Heep**
**The Magician's Birthday**
Bronze, 1972
Roger Dean (Design)
Fin Costello (Photo)

09 APR

**Imha Tarikat**
**Sternenberster**
Lupus Lounge, 2021
Cold Poison (Design)

10 APR

**Graveyard**
Tee Pee Records, 2008
Martin Hultqvist (Design)
Davis (Illustration)

11 APR

**Obelyskkh**
**Hymn To Pan**
Exile on Mainstream Records, 2013
Sebastian Feld (Design)

**12** APR

**Accept**
**Breaker**
Brain, 1981
Accept, Studio Icks (Design)
Stefan Böhle (Photo)

13 APR

**Lucifer Star Machine**
**The Devil's Breath**
Hells Headbangers, 2013
S. Suntharasri (Design)
Matthew Carr (Illustration)

14 APR

**Slayer**
**Hell Awaits**
Metal Blade Records, 1985
Albert Cuellar (Design)

15 APR

**Fragments Of Unbecoming**
**The Art Of Coming Apart**
Cyclone Empire, 2012
Sascha Ehrich (Design)

16 APR

**Mercyful Fate**
**Dead Again**
Metal Blade Records, 1998
Joe Vera (Design)
Kristian Wåhlin (Illustration)

17 APR

**Agressor**
**Neverending Destiny**
Noise International, 1990
Philippe Druillet (Design)

18 APR

**Wolfbrigade**
**Prey To The World**
Agipunk, 2007
Henrik Gallon, Wolfbrigade (Design)
Johan Erkenvåg (Illustration)

# 19 APR

**Spiritual Beggars**
**Mantra III**
Music For Nations, 2015
Mez Meredith (Design)

20 APR

**Magick Touch**
**Heads Have Got To Rock'n'Roll**
Edged Circle Productions, 2020
Olav Iversen (Design)

21 APR

**Gaupa**
**Feberdröm**
Kozmik Artifactz, 2020
Ekaterina Kretiv (Design)

# 22 APR

**Detraktor**
**Full Body Stomp**
Massacre Records, 2022
Cover Artists Unknown

23 APR

**Sodom**
**Persecution Mania**
Steamhammer, 1987
Agentur Schlück (Design)
Johannes Beck (Illustration)

24 APR

**Exhumed**
**Death Revenge**
Relapse Records, 2017
Orion Landau (Design)

25 APR

**The Kovenant**
**Animatronic**
Nuclaer Blast, 1999
Union Design (Design)
Per Heimly (Photo)

26 APR

**Church Of Misery**
**Vol. 1**
Leaf Hound Records, 2007
M-Glue, Tatsuhiko Nonaka (Design)

27 APR

**Kreator**
**Endless Pain**
Noise, 1985
Phil Lawvere (Illustration)

28 APR

**Savatage**
**Sirens**
Par Records, 1983
Jeffrey S. King (Design)

29 APR

**Heaven Shall Burn**
*Veto*
Century Media, 2013
Patrick Wittstock (Design)
Patrick Wittstock (Illustration)

30 APR

**Electric Taurus / Prehistoric Pigs**
Go Down Records, 2014
Cover Artists Unknown

01 MAY

**Obituary**
**Inked In Blood**
Relapse Records, 2014
Andreas Marschall (Design)

02  MAY

**Guns N' Roses**
**Sweet Child O' Mine**
Geffen Records, 1988
ADC Production (Design)
Robert John (Photo)

03 MAY

**Municipal Waste**
**Massive Aggressive**
Earache, 2009
Mark Reategui, Ryan Waste, Tony Foresta (Design)
Andrei Bouzikov (Illustration)

04 MAY

**Tower**
**Tomorrow & Yesterday**
Blasphlegmy, 2019
Zak Penley, Jessica Penley (Design)
Kelsey Henderson (Photo)

05 MAY

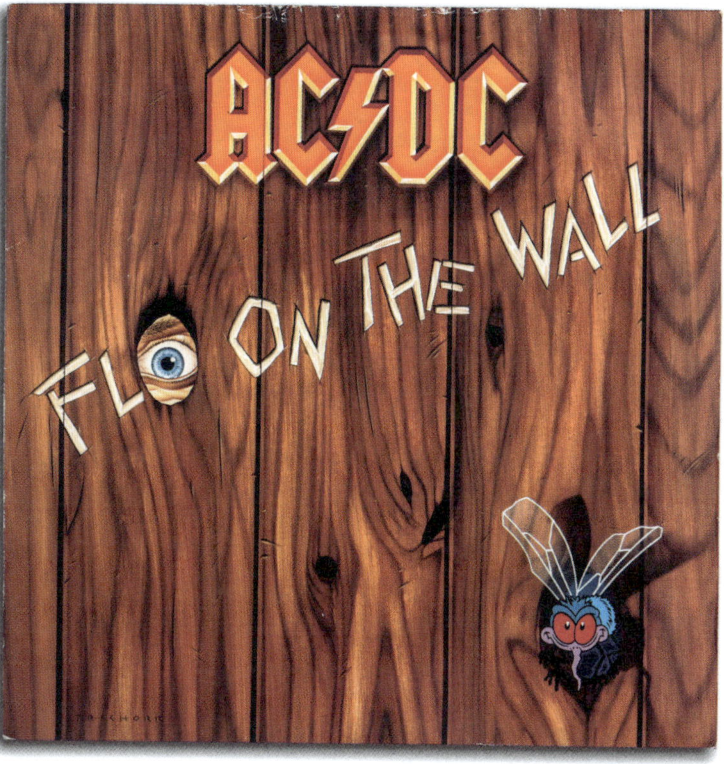

**AC/DC**
**Fly On The Wall**
Albert Productions, 1985
Bob Defrin (Design)
Todd Schorr (Illustration)

06  MAY

**Striker**
**City Of Gold**
Napalm Records, 2014
Cover Artists Unknown

07 MAY

**Night Laser**
**Power To Power**
Out of Line, 2020
Wolfgang "Foto Wolle" Kühnle-RIP (Design)
Wolfgang "Foto Wolle" Kühnle-RIP (Photo)

08 MAY

**Karma To Burn**
**Mountain Czar**
Rodeostar Records, 2016
Alex von Wieding (Design)
Alex von Wieding (Illustration)

**09** MAY

**Bolt Thrower**
**... For Victory**
Earache, 1994
Cover Artists Unknown

# 10 MAY

**Behemoth**
**Evangelion**
Nuclear Blast, 2009
Tomasz Danilowicz (Design)
Tomasz Danilowicz (Illustration)

11  MAY

**Carnivore**
Roadrunner Records, 1985
Seán Taggert, Peter Steele (Design)

**12** MAY

**Alice Cooper**
**Trash**
Epic Records, 1989
David Coleman (Design)
Glen La Ferman (Photo)

13 MAY

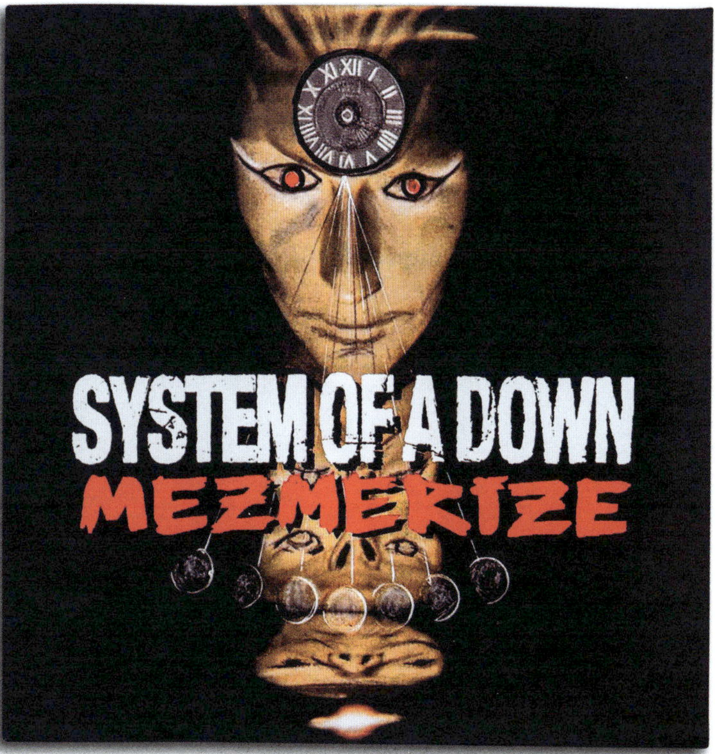

**System Of A Down**
**Mezmerize**
American Recordings, 2005
Brandy Flower, System Of A Down (Design)
Vartan Malakian (Illustration)

14 MAY

**Amon Amarth**
**Fate Of Norns**
Metal Blade Records, 2004
Thomas Ewerhard (Illustration)

## 15 MAY

**Black Sabbath**
**Mob Rules**
Vertigo, 1981
Paul Clark (Illustration)

16 MAY

**The Order Of Israfel**
**Wisdom**
Napalm Records, 2014
Staffan "Brallan" Björck (Design)
Henk Jacobson – Art Of Henk (Illustration)

## 17 MAY

**Mantar**
**The Spell**
Nuclear Blast, 2017
Aron Wiesenfeld (Illustration)

18 MAY

**Devil**
**To The Gallows**
Soulseller Records, 2017
Asgeir Mickelson (Design)
Kim Holm (Illustration)

19 MAY

**Howling Wolves**
JanML Records, 2017
Sebo / Wrathbone Art (Illustration)

20 MAY

**Windhand**
Forcefiled Records, 2012
Anneli Kirby (Design)
Asechiah Bogdan (Illustration)

21 MAY

**Gojira**
**The Link**
Boycott Records, 2013
Joe Duplantier (Illustration)

**22** MAY

**Argus**
**Boldly Stride The Doomed**
Cruz del Sur Music, 2011
Brad Moore (Illustration)

23 MAY

**Judas Priest**
**Killing Machine**
CBS, 1978
Roslav Szaybo (Design)
Bob Elsdale (Photo)

# 24 MAY

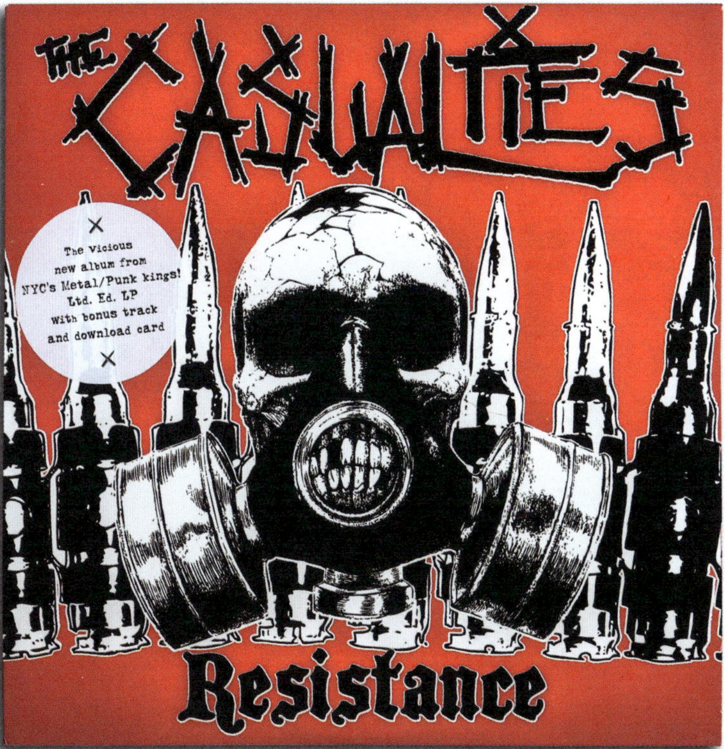

**The Casualties**
**Resistance**
Seasons of Mist, 2012
Brandnewage Design, Mathias (Design)
Halseycaust (Illustration)

25 MAY

**Hypnos**
Morbid Records, 2012
Branca Studio (Design)
Jonna Karlsson (Photo)

26 MAY

**Sanhedrin**
**A Funeral For The World**
Sanhedrin, 2017
Seventhbell Artwork (Design)

## 27 MAY

**Blind Guardian**
**Forgotten Tales**
Nuclaer Blast, 2019
Andreas Marschall (Illustration)

## 28 MAY

**Hällas**
The Sign Records, 2015
Nightjar Illustration (Illustration)

# 29 MAY

**Type O Negative**
**World Coming Down**
Roadrunner Records, 1999
Peter Steele (Design)
Vincent Soyez (Photo)

30 MAY

**Carcass**
**Torn Arteries**
Nuclear Blast, 2021
Zbigniew Bielak (Design)

# 31 MAY

**With The Dead**
Rise Above Records, 2015
L. Dorrian (Design)
Mark Griffiths (Photo)

01 JUN

**Scorpions**
**In Trance**
RCA, 1975
Codesign / Dirichs (Design)
Michael von Gimbut (Photo)

02 JUN

**Incarceration**
**Empiricism**
Dawnbreed Records, 2021
Michel Jonker (Design)

03 JUN

**Megadeth**
**So Far, So Good... So What**
Capitol Records, 1988
Shannon Ward (Design)
Eddie Malluk (Photo)

04 JUN

**Trouble**
**Psalm 9**
Metal Blade Records, 1984
Gary Docken (Design)

05 JUN

**Slayer**
**South Of Heaven**
Def American Recordings, 1988
Douglas Day (Design)
Howard Schwartzberg, Larry Carroll (Illustration)

06 JUN

**Blood Incantation**
**Hidden History Of The Human Race**
Dark Descent Records, 2019
Paul Riedl (Design)
Bruce Pennington (Illustration)

**Fvneral Fvkk**
**Carnal Confessions**
Bleeding Hearst Nihilist Productions, 2019
Irrwisch Artdesign (Design)

## 08 JUN

**UFO**
**Force It**
Chrysalis, 1975
Hipgnosis (Design)

09 JUN

**Saturn**
**Ascending (Live In Space)**
Rise Above Records, 2014
Eric Koerffer & Saturn (Design)

# 10 JUN

**Psychotic Waltz**
**The God-Shaped Void**
Inside Out Music, 2020
Travis Smith (Design)

11 JUN

**Extreme II**
**Pornograffitti (A Funked Up Fairytale)**
A&M Records, 1990
Ioannis, Third Image (Design)
Extreme, Third Image (Illustration)

12 JUN

**The Ossuary**
**Southern Funeral**
Supreme Chaos Records, 2019
Cover Artists Unknown

13 JUN

**Lucifer**
**IV**
Century Media, 2021
Ola Hjelm (Photo)

14 JUN

**Sepultura**
**Roorback**
Steamhammer, 2003
Derek Hess (Design)

# 15 JUN

**Horisont**
**About Time**
Century Media, 2017
Henrik Bastrup Jacobsen (Illustration)

16 JUN

**Pretty Maids**
**Kingmaker**
Soulfood, 2016
Kai Brockschmidt (Design)

17 JUN

**Ancient**
**The Cainian Chronicle**
Flora Records, 2017
Alex Kurtagic (Design)

18 JUN

**Nazareth**
**Hair of the Dog**
Vertigo, 1975
Dave Roe (Illustration)

# 19 JUN

**Fear Factory**
**Obsolete**
Roadrunner Records, 2018
Dave McKean, Fear Factory (Design)
Dave McKean (Photo)

20 JUN

**Black Vulpine**
**Veil Nebula**
Moment of Collapse Records, 2019
Written In Black Designworks (Design)

21 JUN

**Starlight Ritual**
**Sealed In Starlight**
Temple Of Mystery Records, 2021
Undirheimar (Design)

**22** JUN

**Exodus**
**Blood In Blood Out**
Nuclear Blast, 2014
Par Olofsson (Design)

**23** JUN

**Hallow's Eve**
**Tales Of Terror**
Roadrunner Records, 1985
Stacy Anderson (Design)
Randi Hamburg (Illustration)

24 JUN

**Blood Ceremony**
Rise Above Records, 2019
Annick Giroux (Design)
George Barr (Illustration)

25 JUN

**Hexx**
**Under The Spell**
Roadrunner Records, 1986
Guy Aitchison (Illustration)

26 JUN

**Pantera**
**Far Beyond Driven**
EastWest Records America, 1994
Richard Bates (Design)
Darren Crawforth / Geezer (Photo)

27 JUN

**Killswitch Engage**
**The End Of Heartache**
Metal Blade Records, 2020
Mike D'Antonio (Illustration)

28 JUN

**Metallica**
**Creeping Death**
Music For Nations, 1984
Alvin Petty (Illustration)

29 JUN

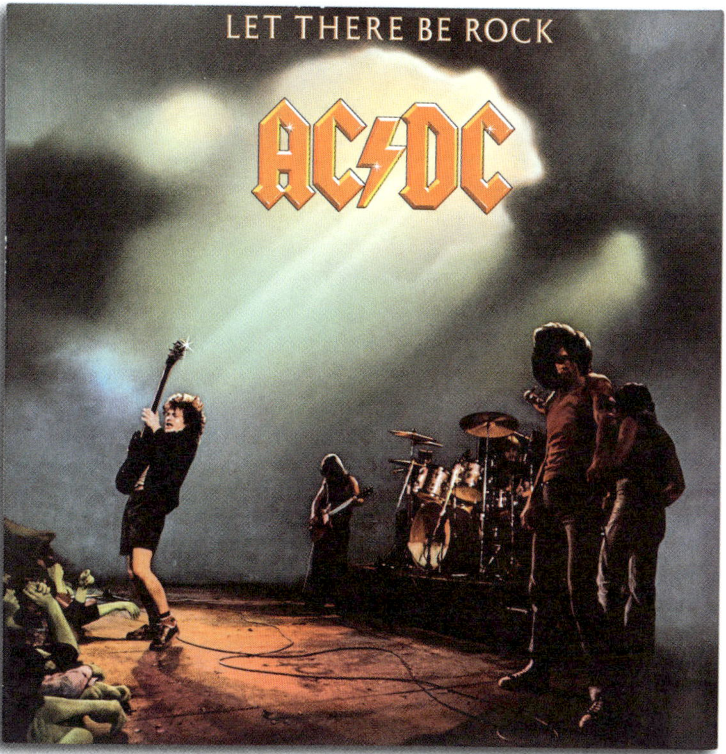

**AC/DC**
**Let There Be Rock**
ATCO Records, 1977
Bob Defrin (Design)

## 30 JUN

**Skeletor**
**Bastards Of The Universe**
Not on Label, 2015
Joost Halbersma (Design)

01 JUL

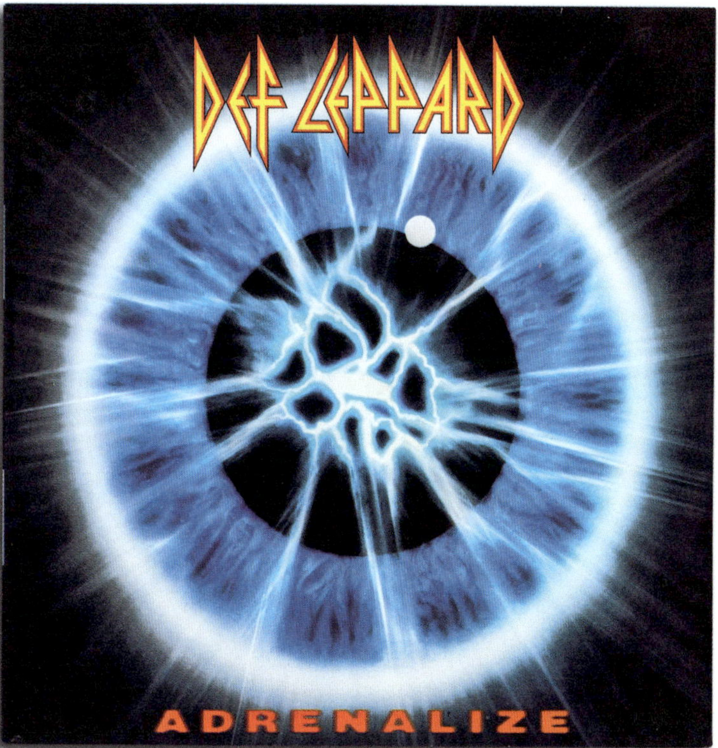

**Def Leppard**
**Adrenalize**
Bludgeon Riffola, 1992
Andie Airfix (Design)
Pamela Springsteen, Ronnie Norton (Photo)

02 JUL

**Gold**
**Optimist**
Váa, 2017
Milena Eva, Thomas Sciarone (Photo)

# 03 JUL

**Celtic Frost**
**Parched With Thirst Am I And Dying**
Noise International, 1992
Istvan Vizner (Design)

04 JUL

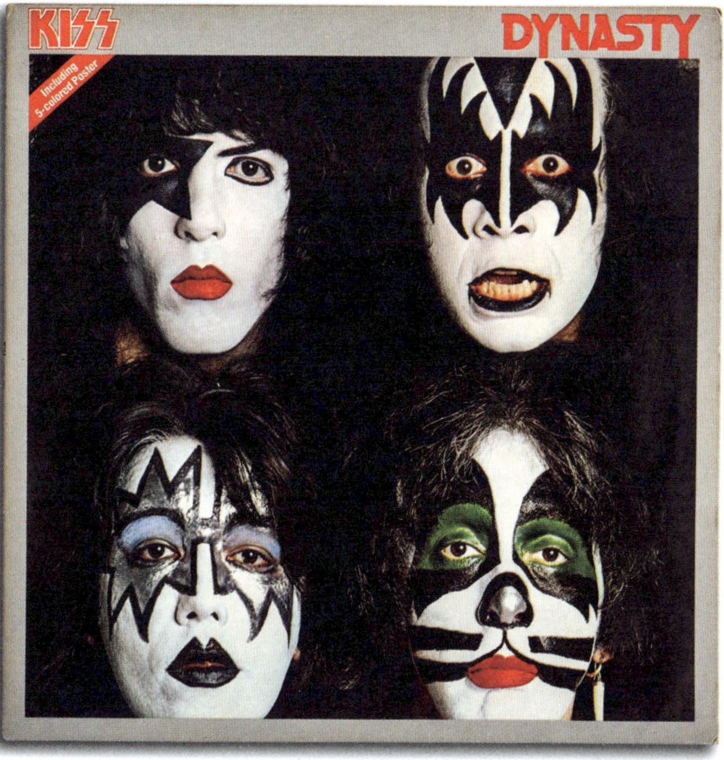

**Kiss**
**Dynasty**
Casablanca, 1979
Howard Marks Advertising, Inc. (Design)
Francesco Scavullo (Photo)

05   JUL

**Benediction**
**Transcend The Rubicon**
Nuclaer Blast, 1993
Dan Seagrave (Design)

06 JUL

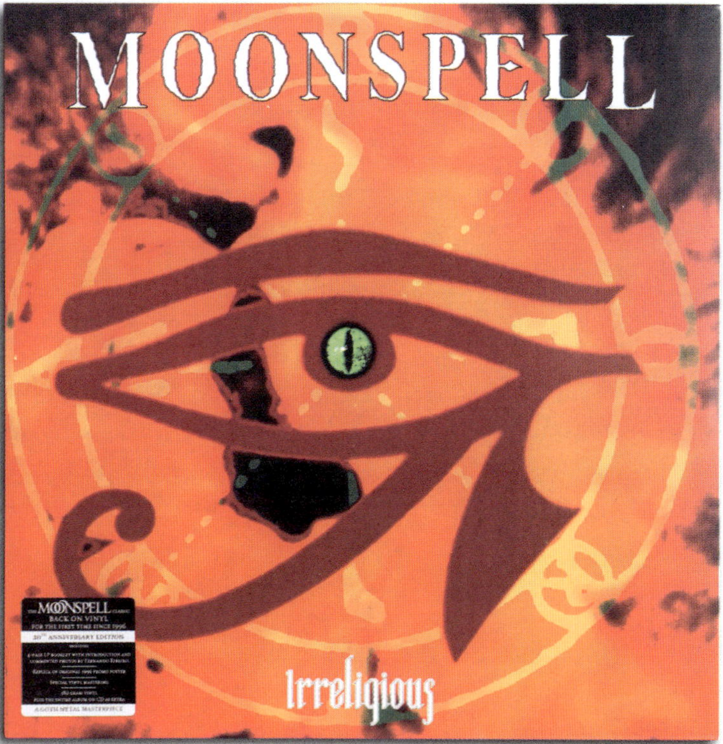

**Moonspell**
**Irreligious**
Century Media, 2016
Carsten Drescher, Moonspell (Design)

07 JUL

**Sacred Reich**
**Heal**
Metal Blade Records, 1996
Brian J Ames (Design)
Max Aguilera Hellweg (Illustration)

08 JUL

**Rob Zombie**
**Hellbilly Deluxe**
Geffen Records, 1998
Lucky Ninja House Of Graphics, Nika, Rob Zombie (Design)
Basil Gogos (Illustration)

# 09    JUL

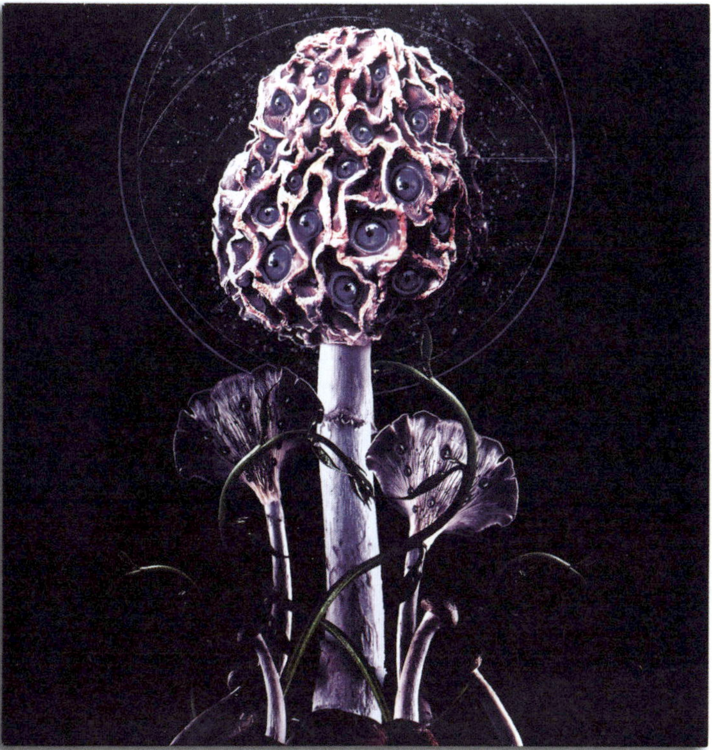

**Blut Aus Nord**
**Hallucinogen**
Debemur Morti Productions, 2019
Endseeker (Design)

10 JUL

**Endsenker**
**Mount Carcass**
Metal Blade Records, 2021
Anditya Dita / Poison Project (Illustration)

**11** JUL

**Kayleth**
**2020 Back To Earth**
Argonauta Records, 2020
Massimo Dalla Valle (Design)

12 JUL

**Heavy Temple**
**Lupi Amoris**
Magnetic Eye Records, 2021
Cover Artists Unknown

13 JUL

**Motörhead**
**Rock'n' Roll**
GWR Records, 1987
John F. McGill (Design)
Joe Petagno (Illustration)

**14** JUL

**Vulture**
**Dealin' Death**
Metal Blade Records, 2021
Cover Artists Unknown

15 JUL

**Riot City**
**Burn The Night**
No Remorse Records, 2019
George Zacharoglou (Design)
Anton Atanasov (Illustration)

 16 JUL

**Helix**
**No Rest For The Wicked**
Capitol Records, 1983
Heather Brown (Design)
S.C. Dean (Photo)

# 17 JUL

**Dr. Living Dead!**
**Radioactive Intervention**
High Roller Records, 2012
Klotterbaronen (Design)

18 JUL

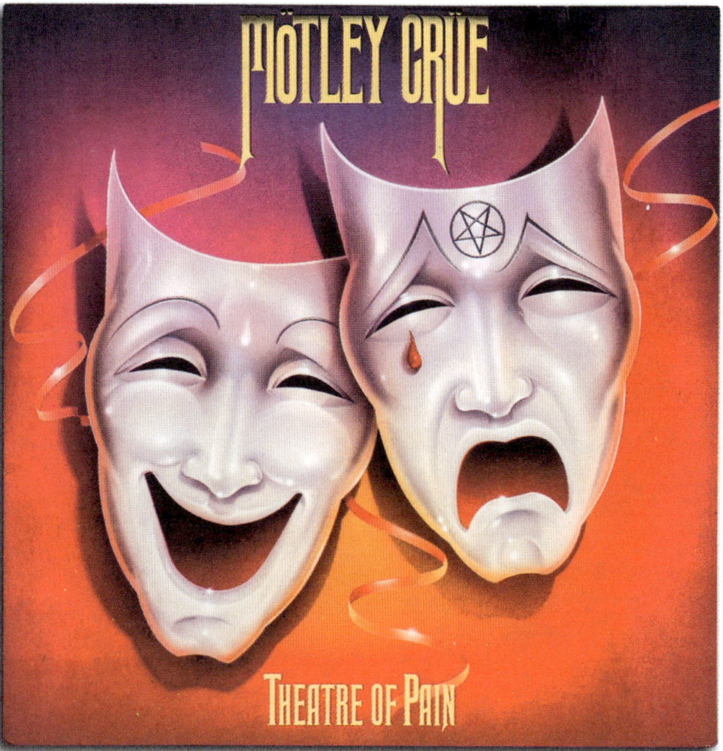

**Mötley Crüe**
**Theatre Of Pain**
Elektra, 1985
Bob Defrin (Design)
Dave Willardson (Illustration)

# 19 JUL

**Cripper**
**Hyëna**
Metal Blade Records, 2014
Cover Artists Unknown

20 JUL

**Life Of Agony**
**River Runs Red**
Roadrunner Records, 1993
Laura Michaels Design (Design)
Joann Daley (Illustration)

21 JUL

**Sick Of It All**
**Last Act Of Defiance**
Century Media, 2014
Ernie Parada (Design)

22 JUL

**High On Fire**
**Snakes For The Divine**
E1 Music, 2010
Arik Roper (Design)

23 JUL

**Demon Head**
**Viscera**
Metal Blade Records, 2021
Cover Artists Unknown

24 JUL

**Soen**
**Imperial**
Silver Lining Music, 2021
Cover Artists Unknown

25 JUL

**Surgical Strike**
**Part Of A Sick World**
Metalville, 2020
Timon Kokott (Design)

26 JUL

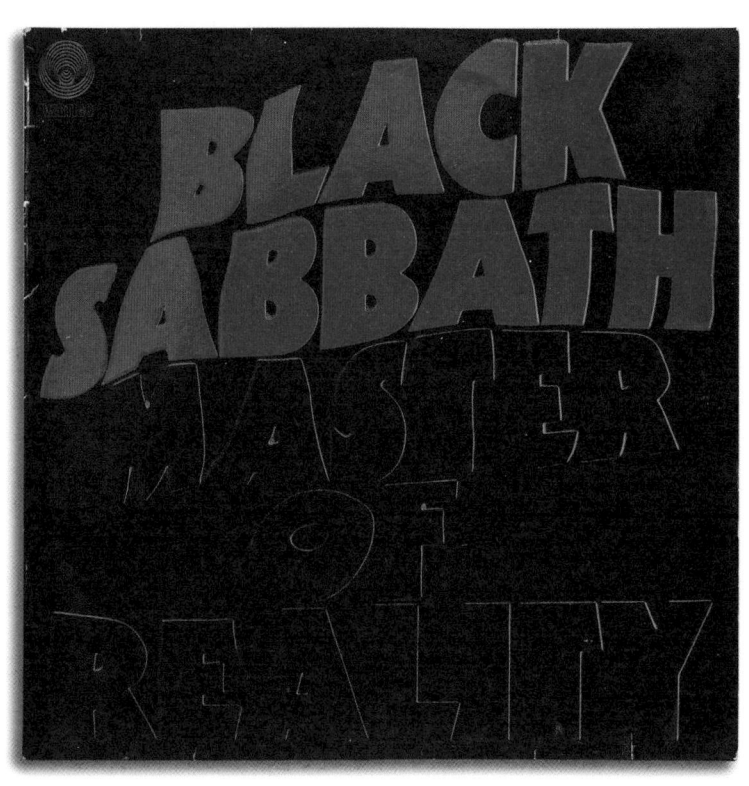

**Black Sabbath**
**Master Of Reality**
Vertigo, 1971
Mike Stanford (Design)

27 JUL

**Dead Lord**
**Surrender**
Century Media, 2020
Hakim Krim (Design)
Kristoffer Axiö (Illustration)

28 JUL

**Mount Atlas**
**Titan**
Daredevil Records, 2017
Alfiandikid (Illustration)

29 JUL

**Iron Maiden**
**Life After Death**
Capitol Records, 1985
Steve "Krusher" Joule (Design)
Derek "R.I.P." Riggs (Illustration)

# 30   JUL

**Amorphis**
**Black Winter Day**
Relapse Records, 1996
Wes Benscoter (Design)

31 JUL

**Freedom**
Not on Label, 2021
Magnus Berglund (Design)
Freedom (Photo)

# 01 AUG

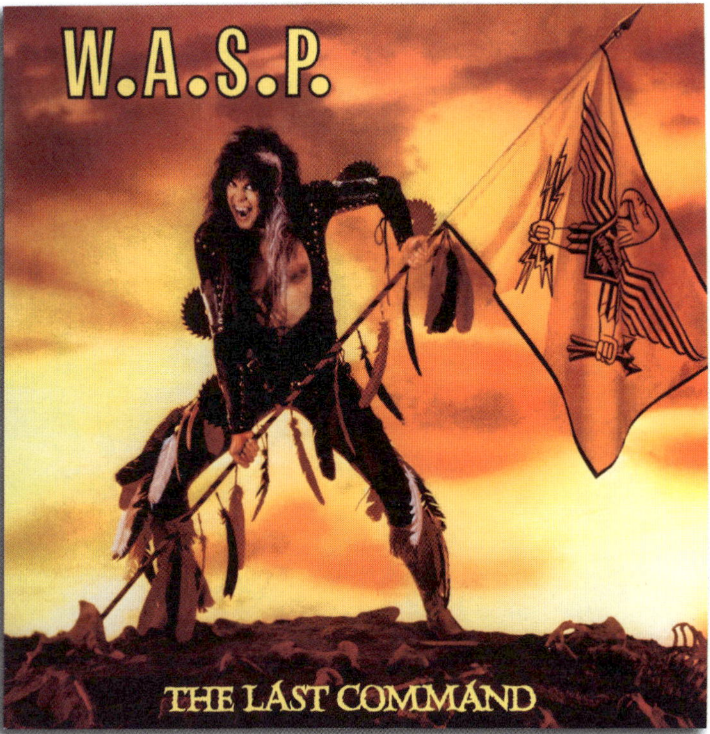

**W.A.S.P.**
**The Last Command**
Capitol Records, 1985
Vigon Seireeni (Design)
Mark "Weiss-Guy" Weiss (Photo)

# 02 AUG

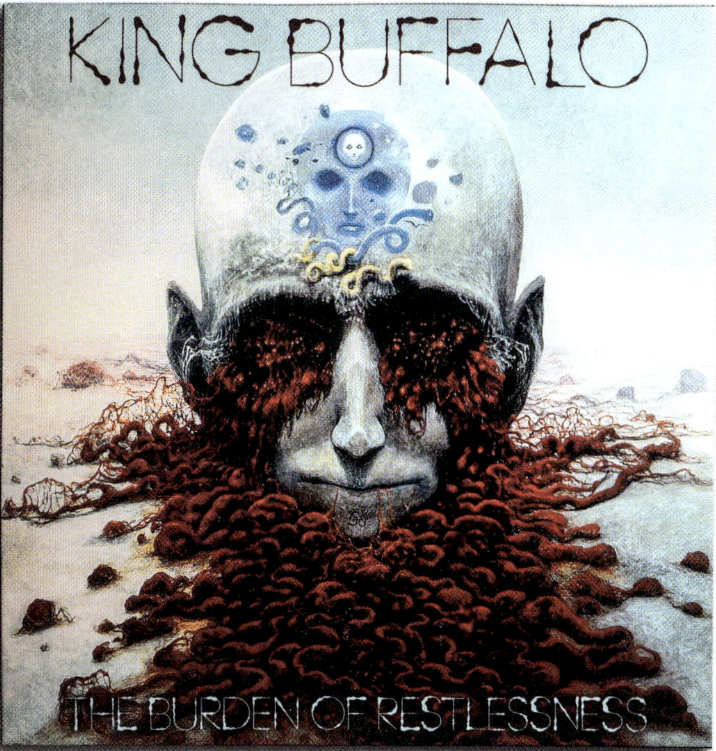

**King Buffalo**
**The Burden Of Restlessness**
King Buffalo Self Release, 2021
Zdislaw Beksinski (Design)
Mike Turzanski (Illustration)

03 AUG

**Tragedian**
**Seven Dimensions**
Pride & Joy Music, 2021
Gabriele Palermo, Rainer Kalwitz (Design)
Piotr Szafraniec (Illustration)

## 04 AUG

**Villagers Of Ioannina City**
**Age Of Aquarius**
Napalm Records, 2020
Fotis Varthis (Design)

# 05 AUG

**Siena Root**
**Different Realities**
Headspin Records, 2009
Christian Olanie (Design)

06 AUG

**Hooded Menace**
**The Tritonus Bell**
Seasons of Mist, 2021
Lasse Pyykkö (Design)
Wes Benscoter (Illustration)

07 AUG

**The Devil's Blood**
**Come, Reap**
Ván, 2008
Thomas Gobauer (Design)

08 AUG

**Speedtrap**
**Powerdose**
Svart Records, 2013
Ville Valavuo (Design)

09 AUG

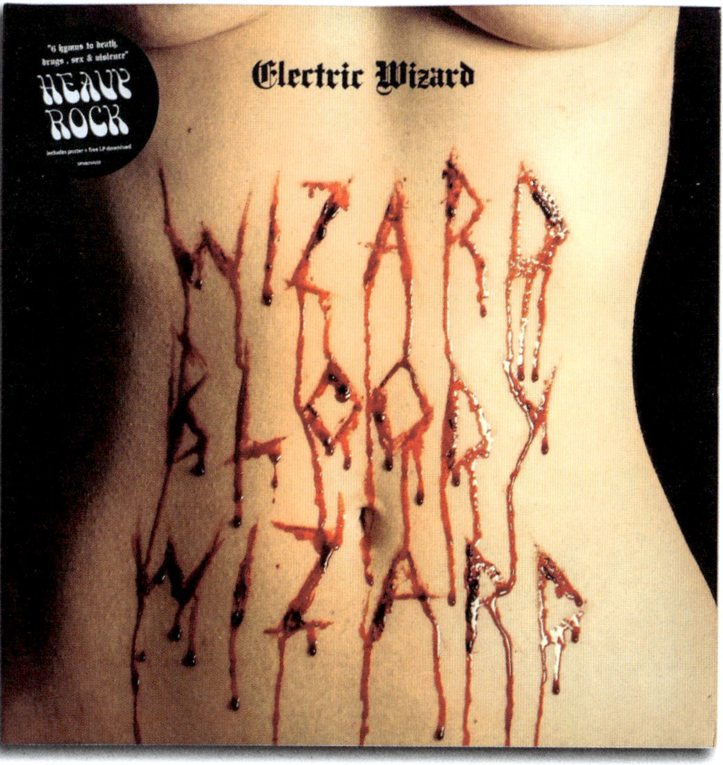

**Electric Wizard**
**Wizard Bloody Wizard**
Witchfinder Records, 2017
Jus Oborn (Design)
Liz Buckingham (Photo)

# 10 AUG

**Black Label Society**
**1919 Eternal Records**
Back on Black, 2011
Peter Tsakiris, Zakk Wylde (Design)
Adam Guyot (Illustration)

**11** AUG

**Status Quo**
**Piledriver**
Vertigo, 1972
Steve Campbell (Photo)

# 12 AUG

**Picture**
**Warhorse**
Pure Steel Records, 2018
Cover Artists Unknown

13 AUG

**Brimstone Coven**
**Black Magic**
Metal Blade Records, 2016
Creighton Hill (Design)

14 AUG

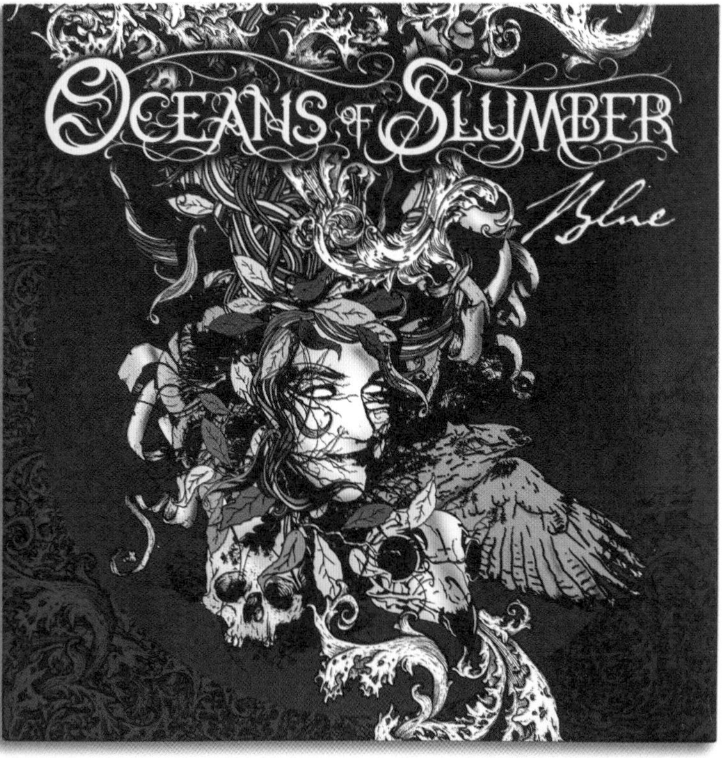

**Oceans Of Slumber**
**Blue**
Century Media, 2015
Cover Artists Unknown

15 AUG

**Morgoth**
**Cursed**
Century Media, 1991
S. Mertens, T. Gielsbach (Design)
Jesus The Conqueror (Illustration)

16 AUG

**Savatage**
**Hall of The Mountain**
Atlantic, 1987
Bob Defrin, Gary Smith (Design)
Gary Smith (Illustration)

17 AUG

**Overkill**
**Under The Influence**
Megaforce Worldwide, 1988
Steve Fastner (Design)

18 AUG

**Ghost**
**If You Have Ghost**
Republic Records, 2013
Mattias Frisk (Design)

19 AUG

**Amon Amarth**
**Jomsviking**
Metal Blade Records, 2016
Tom Thiel (Design)
Garip Jensen (Illustration)

20 AUG

**Kavrila**
**Mor**
Narshardaa Records, 2021
The Bujack Family (Design)
M.Karanastassis (Illustration)

21 AUG

**Havok**
**Time Is Up**
Restricted Release, 2011
Halseycaust (Design)

22 AUG

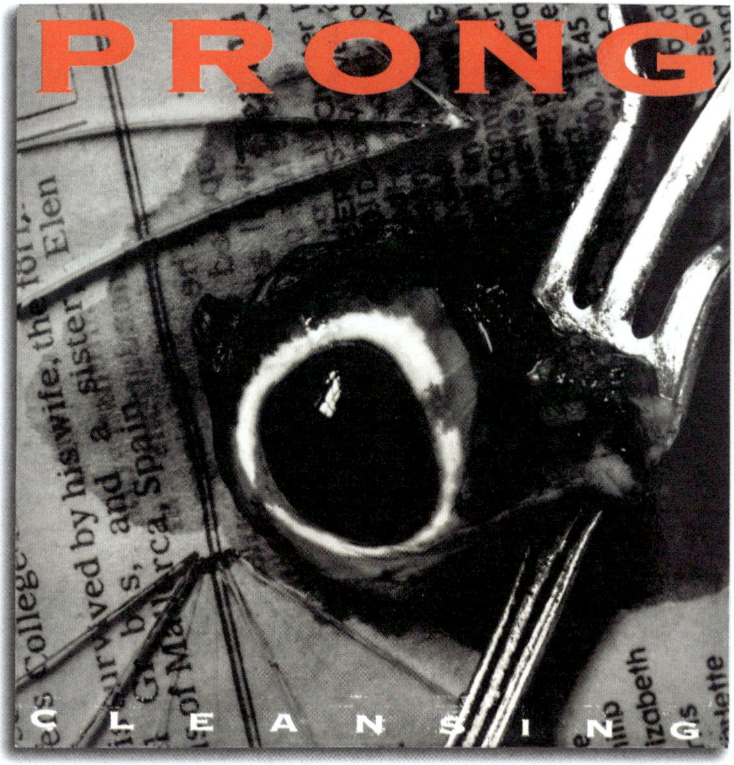

**Prong**
**Cleansing**
Epic, 1994
Ken Schles (Photo)

23 AUG

**Siberian Meat Grinder**
**Metal Bear Stomp**
Destiny Records, 2017
Vladimir Siberian (Design)
Sean Taggart (Illustration)

24 AUG

**Exhumation**
**Eleventh Formulae**
Pulverised Records, 2020
Cover Artists Unknown

25 AUG

**Dawn Of Obliteration**
**Ruins**
Lycanthropic Chants, 2021
Finadesigns (Design)
Rotter (Illustration)

26 AUG

**Napalm Death**
**Fear, Emptiness, Despair**
Earache, 1994
Graham Humphreys (Design)

# 27 AUG

**Benediction**
**The Grand Leveller**
Nuclaer Blast, 1991
Repro Desaster (Design)
Bob Eggleton (Illustration)

28 AUG

**Razor**
**Violent Restitution**
Fringe Product, 1988
Visual Mix, Kitchener (Design)

29 AUG

**Grave Digger**
**The Reaper**
GUN, 1993
Petrus Lohdograficus (Design)
Peter Dell (Illustration)

30 AUG

**Space Chaser**
**Decapitron**
This Charming Man Records, 2020
Basil Wrathbone (Illustration)

31 AUG

**Slayer**
**Live Undead**
Metal Blade Records, 1987
Albert Cuellar (Design)

01 SEP

**Vojd**
**The Outer Ocean**
High Roller Records, 2018
Cover Artists Unknown

02 SEP

**Orchid**
**Heretic**
Nuclear Blast, 2012
Bud Sypeck, Theo Mindell (Design)

03 SEP

**Trinitas**
War Anthem Records, 2019
Cover Artists Unknown

04 SEP

**Tankard**
**The Morning After / Alien**
Nuclear Blast, 1988
Buffo Schnädelbach (Design)
Becker-Derouet, Sebastian Krüger (Illustration)

05 SEP

**Hangman's Chair / Greenmachine**
**Split**
Music Fear Satan, 2017
Cover Artists Unknown

# 06 SEP

**Earthless**
**Live At Freak Valley 2015**
Rock Freaks Records, 2017
Mr. Frumpy (Design)

# 07 SEP

**Orange Goblin**
**A Eulogy For The Damned**
Back on Black, 2012
Jimbob Isaac (Design)

08 SEP

**Vampire**
**Cimmerian Shade**
Century Media, 2015
Cover Artists Unknown

09 SEP

**Kadavar**
**The Isolation Tapes**
Roboter Records, 2020
Sharlach (Illustration)

10 SEP

Admiral Sir Cloudeley Shovell
Keep It Greasy!
Rise Above Records, 2016
Mark Richards (Photo)

11 SEP

**Ghastly**
**Mercurial Passages**
20 Buick Spin, 2021
Chimère Noire (Design)
Riikka Pesonen (Illustration)

12 SEP

**Pestilence**
**Testimony Of The Ancients**
R/C Records, 1991
Patricia Mooney (Design)
Dan SeaGrave (Illustration)

13 SEP

**Unleashed**
**Where No Life Dwells**
Century Media, 1991
Axel Hermann (Design)
Axel Hermann (Illustration)

# 14 SEP

**Iron Maiden**
**Powerslave**
EMI, 1984
Derek Riggs, Iron Maiden, Rod Smallwood (Design)
Derek "The Master" Riggs (Illustration)

15 SEP

**Sacred Reich**
**The American Way**
Roadracer Records, 1990
Paul Stottler (Design)

16 SEP

**Hail The Void**
Phobiact Records, 2012
Jim Geigerich (Design)

# 17 SEP

**Bastardur**
**Satan's Loss Of Son**
Season of Mist, 2021
Fannar Öm Kansson (Design)
Adrien Bousson (Illustration)

18 SEP

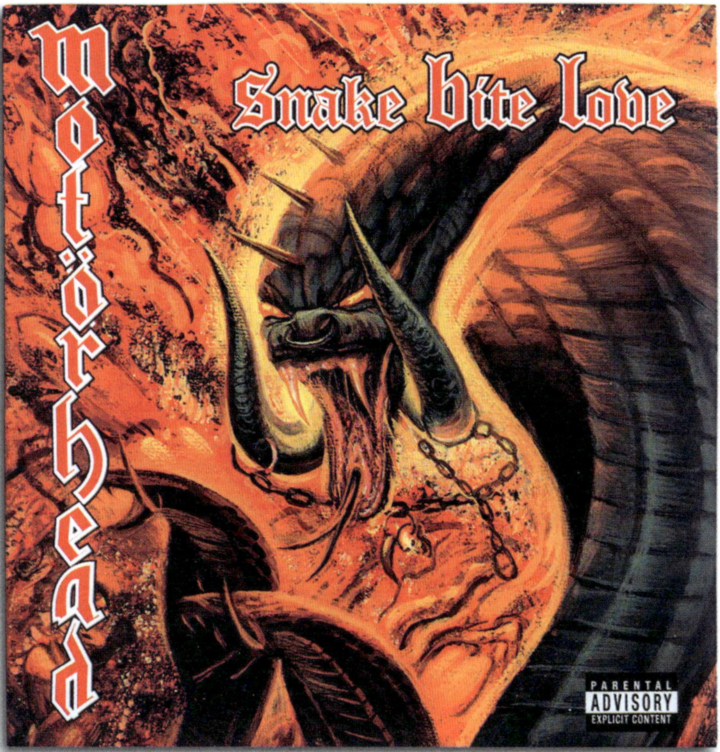

**Motörhead**
**Snake Bite Love**
Steamhammer, 1988
Joe Petagno (Illustration)

19 SEP

**Deep Purple**
**Burn**
Purple Records, 1974
Fin Costello (Photo)

20 SEP

**Nine Inch Nails**
**The Downward Spiral**
Island Records, 1994
Gary Talpas (Design)
Russell Mills (Photo)

21 SEP

**Kreator**
**Enemy Of God**
Steamhammer, 2005
Joachim Luetke (Design)

22 SEP

**Powergame**
**Slaying Gods**
Iron Shield Records, 2022
Kostas Tsiakos (Illustration)

23 SEP

**Tomb Mold**
**Planetary Clairvoyance**
20 Buick Spin, 2019
Lucas Korte (Design)
Jesse Jacobi (Illustration)

24 SEP

**Cirith Ungol**
**Frost And Fire**
Liquide Flame Records, 1981
Warren Archer (Design)
Michael Whelan (Illustration)

25 SEP

**Robert Pehrsson's Humbucker**
**Out Of The Dark**
High Roller Records, 2019
Robert Pehrsson (Design)
Eneko Garcia Ureta (Illustration)

## 26 SEP

**High Spirits**
**Motivator**
High Roller Records, 2016
Alex / Zeichentier.com (Design)
Alexander von Wieding (Illustration)

27 SEP

**Testament**
**The Legacy**
Megaforce Worldwide, 1987
Alexis Olson (Design)
Bill Benson (Illustration)

28 SEP

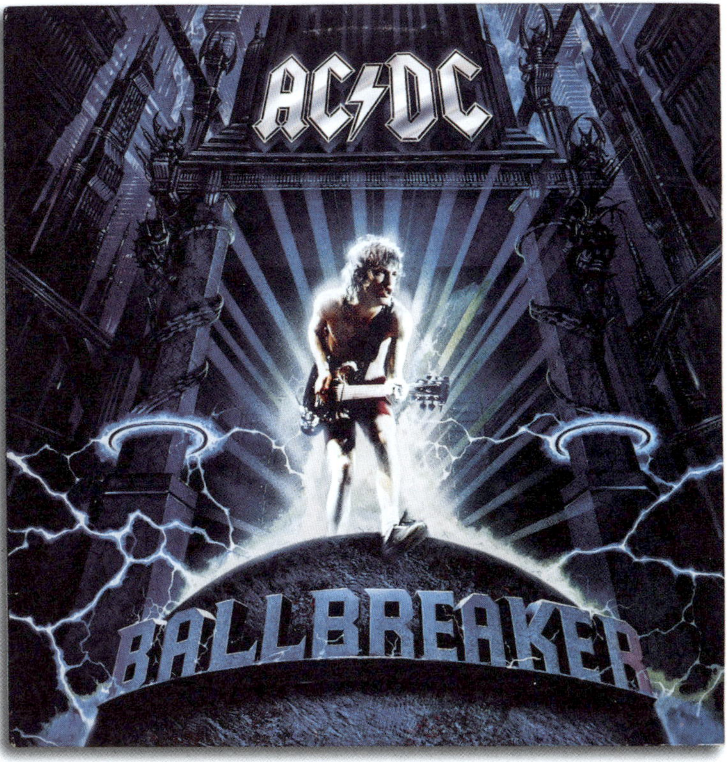

**AC/DC**
**Ballbreaker**
EastWest Records America, 1995
Phil Heffernan (Design)

29 SEP

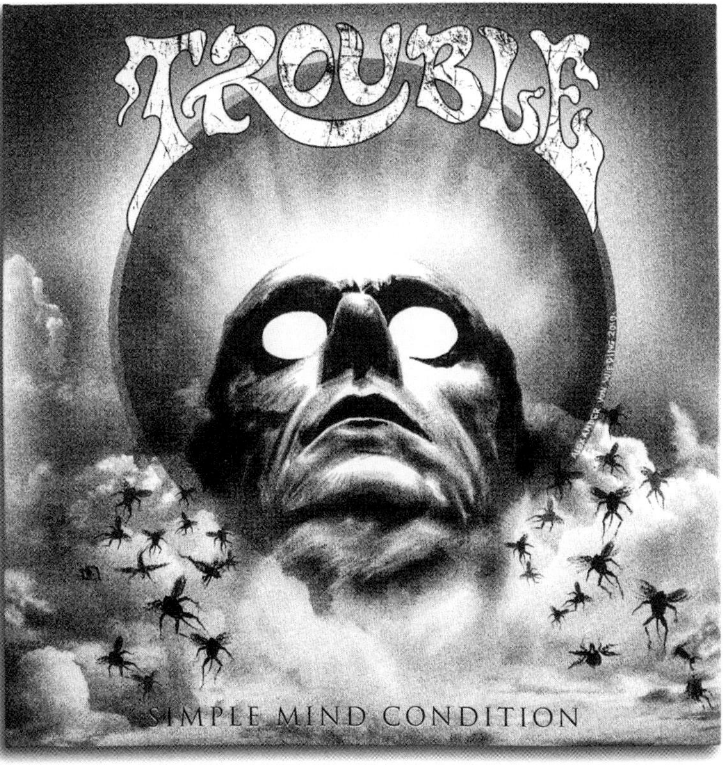

**Trouble**
**Simple Mind Condition**
FRW Music, 2009
Alexander Von Wieding (Design)

30 SEP

**Welcome Dystopia**
**Solitude**
Not on Label, 2021
Tammy Maas (Design)
Visha Goel (Illustration)

# 01 OCT

**Skid Row**
**Slave To The Grind**
Atlantic, 1991
Bob Defrin (Design)
David Bierk (Illustration)

02 OCT

**Black Viper**
**Hellions Of Fire**
High Roller Records, 2018
Rolf Kristian Valbo (Design)
H. Johansson (Illustration)

## 03 OCT

**Smoulder**
**Dream Quest Ends**
Cruz del Sur Music, 2020
Obscure Visions (Design)
Michael Whelan (Illustration)

04 OCT

**Midnight**
**Berlin Is Burning**
Nuclear War Now! Productions, 2009
Cover Artists Unknown

05 OCT

**Green Lung**
**Free The Witch**
Kozmik Artifactz, 2019
Tom Templar (Design)
Richard Wells (Illustration)

## 06 OCT

**Scorched Oak**
**Withering Earth**
Not on Label, 2020
Maciej Kamuda (Design)

**Trouble**
**Manic Frustration**
Def American Recordings, 1992
Kim Champagne (Design)
Jean-Francois Podevin (Illustration)

## 08 OCT

**Century**
**Demo MMXX**
Gates Of Hell Records, 2021
Staffan Tegnér (Design)

## 09 OCT

**Judas Priest**
**Ram It Down**
CBS, 1988
Mark Wilkinson (Design)

10 OCT

**Static-X**
**Wisconsin Death Trip**
Music on Vinyl, 2015
Steve Gerdes (Design)
Exum (Photo)

# 11 OCT

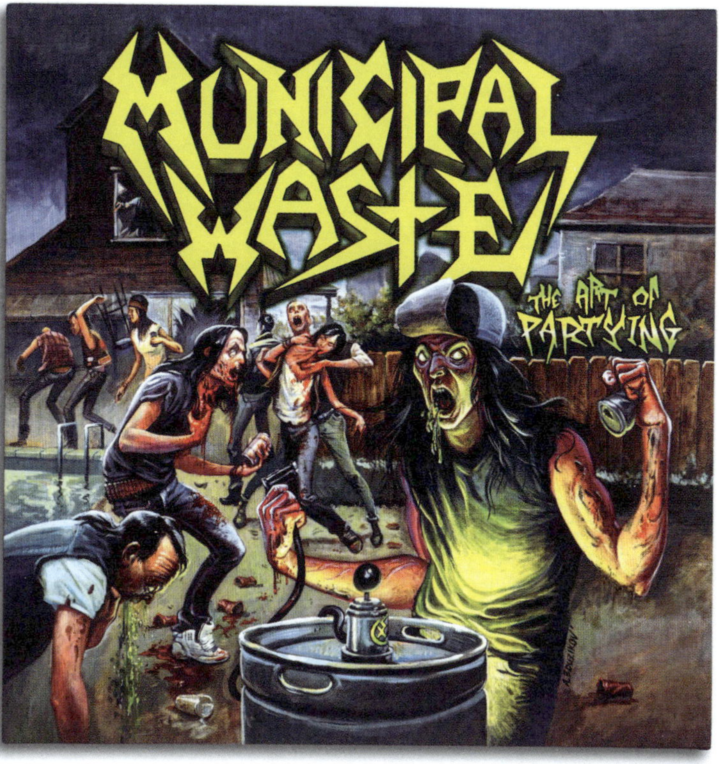

**Municipal Waste**
**The Art Of Partying**
Earache, 2007
Mark Reategui, Municipal Waste (Design)
Andrei Bouzikov (Illustration)

# 12 OCT

**Spellbook**
**Magick & Mischief**
Cruz del Sur Music, 2020
Chad Keith (Illustration)

13 OCT

**Monster Magnet**
**Spine Of God**
Go Get Organized, 1991
Alexander von Wiedig (Design)
Pakito Bolino (Illustration)

# 14 OCT

**Black Sabbath**
**Heaven & Hell**
Vertigo, 1980
Richard Seireeni (Design)
Lynn Curlee (Illustration)

# 15 OCT

**Pyogenesis**
**Twinaleblood**
Nuclear Blast, 1995
Pyogenesis (Design)

# 16 OCT

**The Ocean**
**Precambrian**
Pelagic Records, 2008
Martin Kvamme (Design)

17 OCT

**Jess & The Ancient Ones**
**Astral Sabbat**
Svart Records, 2013
Jari Nieminen (Design)
Nightjar Illustration (Illustration)

18 OCT

**Chapel Of Disease**
**... And As We Have Seen The Storm**
Ván, 2018
Timo Ketola (Design)

19 OCT

**Unleashed**
**No Sign Of Life**
Napalm Records, 2021
Joakim Sterner (Design)
Pär Olofsson (Illustration)

20 OCT

**Screamer**
**Highway Of Heroes**
The Sign Records, 2019
Branca Studio (Design)
Matthias Karlsson, SLB Foto

21 OCT

**Galaxy**
**On The Shore Of Life**
Dying Victims Productions, 2021
Killustrate Illustrations (Design)

## 22 OCT

**My Dying Bride**
**The Ghost Of Orion**
Nuclaer Blast, 2020
Eliran Kantor (Design)

23 OCT

**Odcult**
**Into The Earth**
Mighty Music, 2018
Robin Gnista (Design)

**24** OCT

**Zakk Sabbath**
**Live In Detroit**
Southern Lord, 2017
Samantha Muljat (Design)
Samantha Muljat (Photo)

# 25 OCT

**The Devil's Blood**
**The Thousandfold Epicentre**
Ván, 2011
Druckwerkstatt (Design)
N(obody)'s Fool, Sitis Aeterna (Illustration)

26 OCT

**Dismember**
**Like An Ever Flowing Stream**
Nuclear Blast, 1991
Nicke Andersson (Design)
Dean Seegrave (Illustration)

# 27 OCT

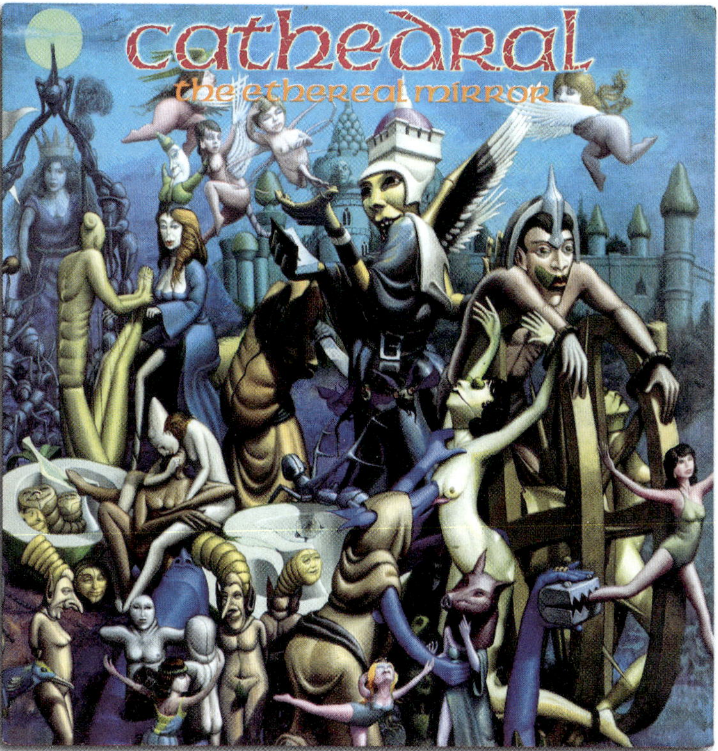

**Cathedral**
**The Ethereal Mirror**
Earache, 1993
Village East (Design)
Dave Patchett (Illustration)

28 OCT

**Mammoth Mammoth**
**Vol. II – Mammoth**
Spinning Goblin Productions, 2013
The Sharp Brothers (Design)

29 OCT

**Overkill**
**Taking Over**
Atlantic, 1987
Christie Mullen, Mike Vayenes, Ron Akiyama (Photo)

30 OCT

**Helloween**
**Dr. Stein**
Noise International, 1987
R. Limb Schnoor (Design)
Frederick Moulaert (Illustration)

31 OCT

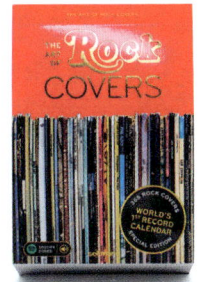
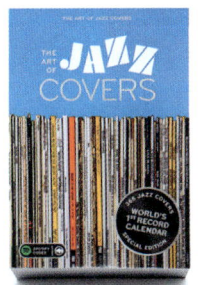
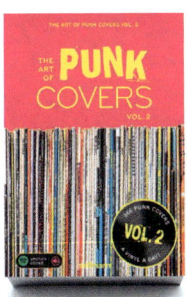
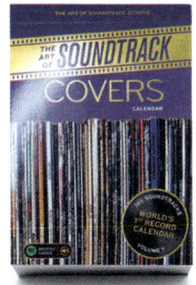
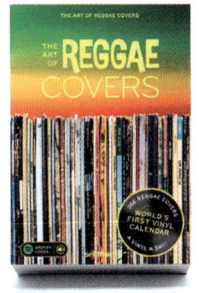
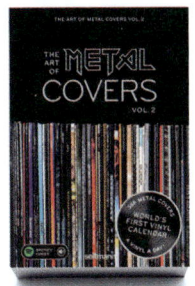

# www.seltmannpublishers.com
Worldwide shipping, free within Germany

**Ace Frehley**
**Frehley's Comet**
WEA, 1987
Bob Defrin (Design)

01 NOV

**Havok**
**Conformicide**
Century Media, 2017
Halsey Swain (Design)

02 NOV

**Obituary**
**World Demise**
Roadrunner Records, 1994
Laura Michaels (Design)
Trevor Peres (Illustration)

03 NOV

**Biohazard**
**Urban Discipline**
Roadrunner Records, 1992
Bryan Thatcher (Design)
Ursula Coyote (Photo)

04 NOV

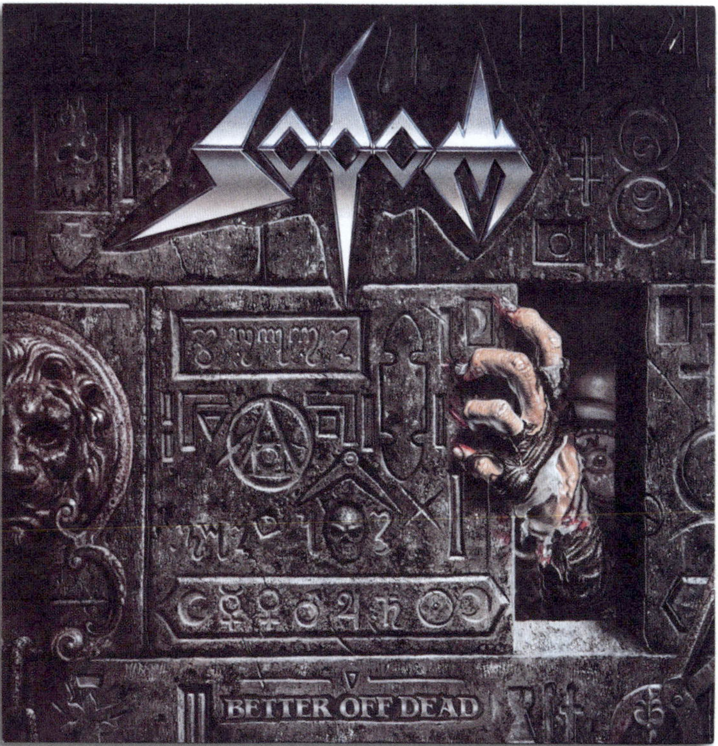

**Sodom**
**Better Off Dead**
Steamhammer, 1990
De Sign Gmbh (Design)
Andreas Marschall (Illustration)

05 NOV

**Geezer Butler**
**Plastic Planet**
BMG, 2020
Greg Knoll, Hugh Gilmour (Design)
Mandie Long (Illustration)

06 NOV

**Slipknot**
**Vol. 3: The Subliminal Verses**
Roadrunner Records, 2004
Michael Boland (Design)
Michael Shawn Crahan (Photo)

07 NOV

**In Flames**
**Whoracle**
Nuclaer Blast, 1997
Andreas Marschall (Illustration)

08 NOV

**Avatarium**
Nuclaer Blast, 2013
Erik Rovanperä (Design)

**09** NOV

**Ophis**
**Withered Shades**
Frontcore Records, 2015
Dušan Bělohlávek (Design)

# 10 NOV

**Entombed**
**Clandestine**
Earache, 1992
Dan Seagrave (Design)
Guerilla Art (Illustration)

11 NOV

**Galactic Superlords**
**Freight Train**
Rockfreak Records, 2020
Solomacello (Illustration)

**12** NOV

**Mount Atlas**
**Mistress**
H42 Records, 2019
Headbanger Design (Design)
Alfiandikid (Illustration)

13 NOV

**Svartanatt**
The Sign Records, 2016
Branca Studio (Design)

14 NOV

**Dead City Ruins**
Metalville, 2014
Beek (Design)
Nick Rutherford (Illustration)

15 NOV

**Death Penalty**
Rise Above Records, 2014
L. Dorrian (Design)
Michelle Nocon (Illustration)

**Savage Master**
**Myth, Magic And Steel**
Shadow Kingdom Records, 2019
Annick Giroux (Design)
Mike Hoffmann (Illustration)

17 NOV

**Demonical**
**Servants Of The Unlight**
Cyclone Empire, 2008
Twilight13Media (Design)
Babalon Graphics (Illustration)

# 18 NOV

**Blues Pills**
Nuclear Blast, 2014
Kiryk Drewinski (Design)
Marijke Koger-Dunham (Illustration)

19 NOV

**The Flight Of Sleipnir**
**Eventide**
Eisenwald, 2021
David Csicsely (Design)

20 NOV

**Electric Sun**
**Earthquake**
Brain, 1979
Monika Dannemann (Design)
Monika Dannemann (Illustration)

21 NOV

**Tiamat**
**The Astral Sleep**
Century Media, 1991
Kristian Wåhlin (Illustration)

22 NOV

**Hazemaze**
**The Paranoid Sessions**
Interstellar Smoke Records, 2021
Cover Artists Unknown

# 23 NOV

**Iron Maiden**
**Fear Of The Dark**
EMI, 1992
Melvyn Grant (Illustration)

# 24   NOV

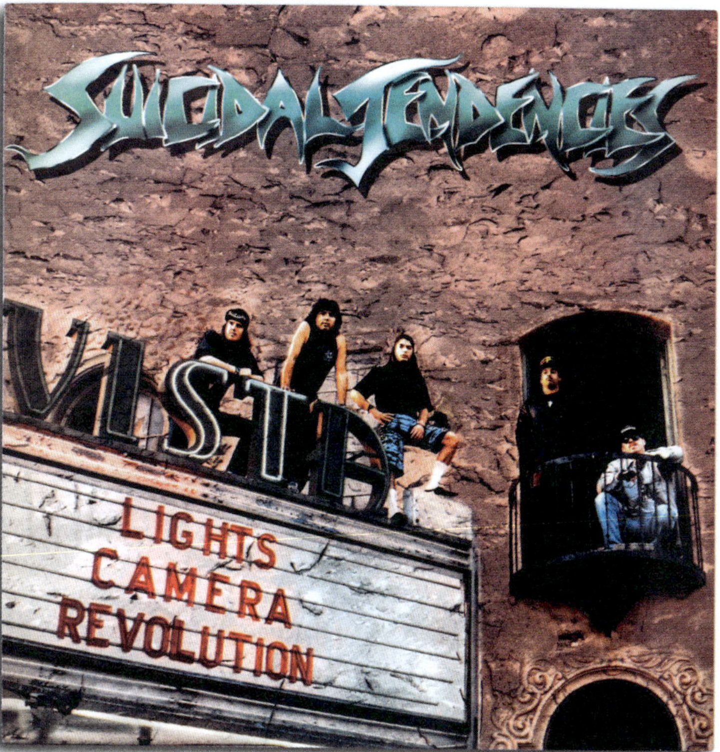

**Suicidal Tendencies**
**Lights, Camera, Revolution**
Epic, 1990
Joel Zimmerman (Design)
Dean Freeman (Photo)

25 NOV

**Slayer**
**Reign In Blood**
Def Jam Recordings, 1986
Stephen Byram (Design)
Larry W. Carroll (Illustration)

26 NOV

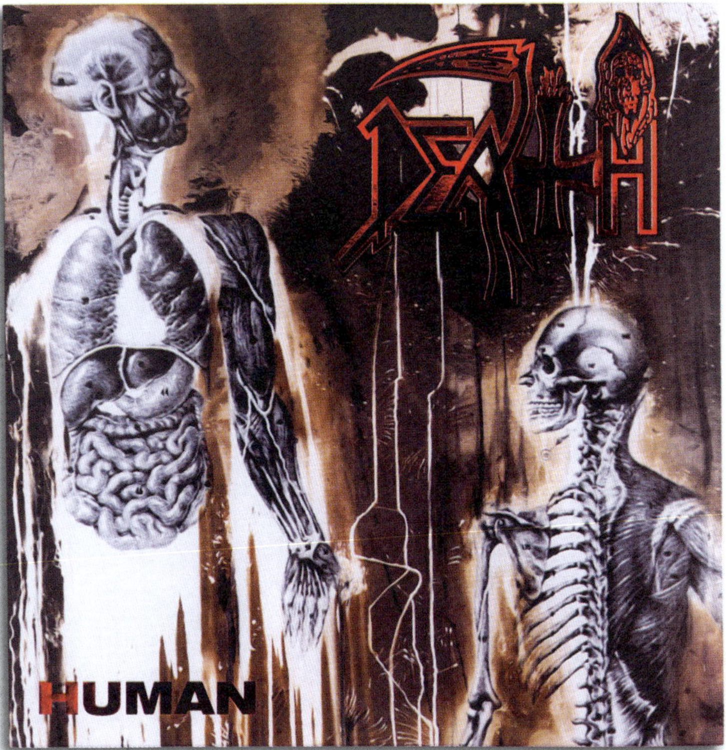

**Death**
**Human**
R/C Records, 1991
David Bett (Design)
René Miville (Illustration)

# 27 NOV

**Mass Hysteria**
**L'Armée Des Ombres**
Verycords, 2012
Eric Canto (Design)
Eric Canto, Juha Arvid Helminen (Photo)

28 NOV

**Pantera**
**Vulgar Display Of Power**
PWL International, 1992
Bob Defrin (Design)
Brad Guice (Photo)

29 NOV

**Children Of Technology**
**Written Destiny**
Hells Headbangers, 2020
Cover Artists Unknown

30 NOV

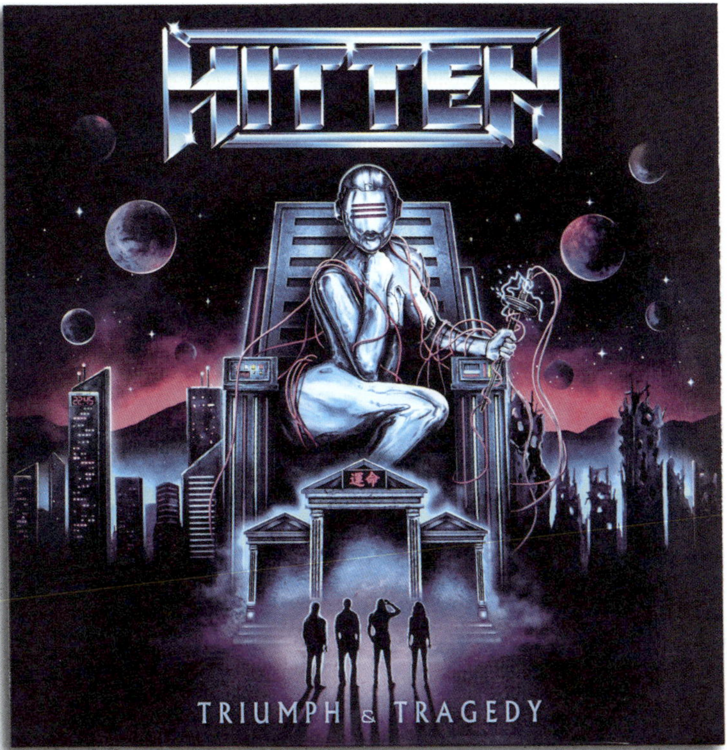

**Hitten**
**Triumph & Tragedy**
High Roller Records, 2021
Marc Schoenbach – Sadist Art Design (Design)

# 01 DEC

**Butterfly**
**Doorways Of Time**
High Voltage Records, 2020
Scott McMahon (Design)
Rodney Matthews (Illustration)

02 DEC

**Deep Purple**
**Machine Head**
Warner Bros. Records, 1972
John Coletta, Roger Glover (Design)
Shepard Sherbell (Photo)

03 DEC

**The Almighty**
**Just Add Life**
Crysalis, 1996
Jon Crossland, Storm Thorgerson (Design)
Rupert Truman, Tony May (Photo)

04  DEC

**Fear Factory**
**Soul Of A New Machine**
Roadrunner Records, 1992
Satok Lrak (Design)
Joe Lance (Photo)

05  DEC

# Perfect gifts.

**www.seltmannpublishers.com**
Worldwide shipping, free within Germany

**Clutch**
**Blast Tyrant**
Weathermaker Music, 2011
Nick Lakiotes (Design)
Chon Hernandez (Illustration)

06 DEC

**Darkthrone**
**Ravishing Grimness**
Moonfog Productions, 1999
Bernt B. Ottem, Moonfog, Nocturnal Cult (Design)

07 DEC

**Heidevolk**
**Uit Oude Grond**
Napalm Records, 2010
Cover Artists Unknown

08 DEC

**Night Viper**
**Exterminator**
Listenable Records, 2017
Staffan "Brallan" Björck (Design)
Karmazid (Illustration)

09 DEC

**Megaton Sword**
**Blood Hails Steel – Steel Hails Fire**
Dying Victims Productions, 2020
Harvest Of Eyes (Design)
Adam Burke (Illustration)

# 10 DEC

**Skid Row**
**Slave To The Grind**
Atlantic, 1991
Bob Defrin (Design)
David Bierk (Illustration)

11 DEC

**Horisont**
**Odyssey**
Rise Above Records, 2015
Henrik Jacobson (Design)

12 DEC

**Agressor**
**Towards Beyond**
Season of Mist, 2021
Headquaters (Design)
Dennis Zappa (Illustration)

13 DEC

**Kiss**
**Love Gun**
Casablanca, 1977
Dennis Woloch (Design)
Ken Kelly (Illustration)

14 DEC

**D.R.I.**
**Thrash Zone**
Metal Blade Records, 1989
Sam Leyja (Design)

# 15 DEC

**Metallica**
**Ride The Lightning**
Megaforce Records, 1984
Metallica (Design)
Ad Artists (Illustration)

16 DEC

**Annihilator**
**Alice In Hell**
Roadrunner Records, 1989
Jeff, Feet (Design)
Len Rooney Creative (Illustration)

17 DEC

**The Neptune Power Federation**
**Memoirs Of A Rat Queen**
Erotic Volcano Records, 2019
Mike Foxall (Design)
Mike Foxall (Illustration)

18 DEC

**Voivod**
**Dimension Hatröss**
Noise International, 1988
Michel Langevin (Design)
Michel Langevin (Illustration)

# 19 DEC

**Ash Return**
**The Sharp Blade Of Integrity**
Swell Greek Records, 2020
Frank Kurowski (Design)

20 DEC

**Paradise Lost**
**One Second**
Music For Nations, 1997
Design Ministry (Design)
Ross Halfin (Illustration)

21 DEC

**Trial**
**Motherless**
Metal Blade Records, 2017
Cover Artists Unknown

22 DEC

**Arch Enemy**
**Khaos Legions**
Century Media, 2021
Brent Elliott White (Design)

23 DEC

**Devil's Witches**
**The Devil's Witches Christmas Special Vol. 1**
Majestic Mountain Records, 2021
Cover Artists Unknown

24 DEC

**Bad News**
**Cashing In On Christmas**
EMI, 1987
Phil Davis (Illustration)

# 25 DEC

**Bathory**
Black Mark Production, 1984
Ace Spunky Black Spade, Quorthon (Design)

# 26 DEC

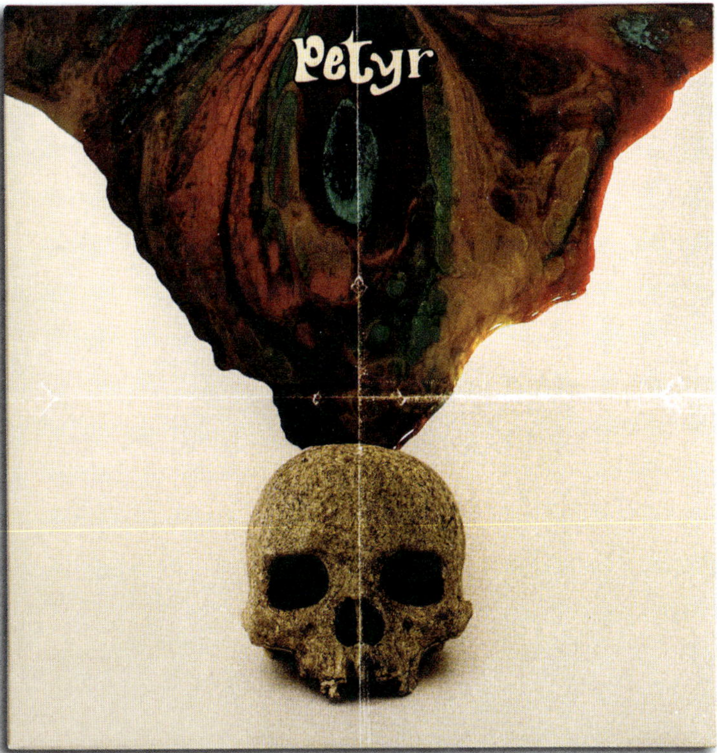

**Petyr**
**Smolyk**
Outer Battery Records, 2018
Dana Trippe (Design)

27 DEC

**Motörhead / Ozzy Osbourne**
**Hellraiser**
Epic, 2021
Frank Harkins (Design)
Steven Payne (Photo)

28 DEC

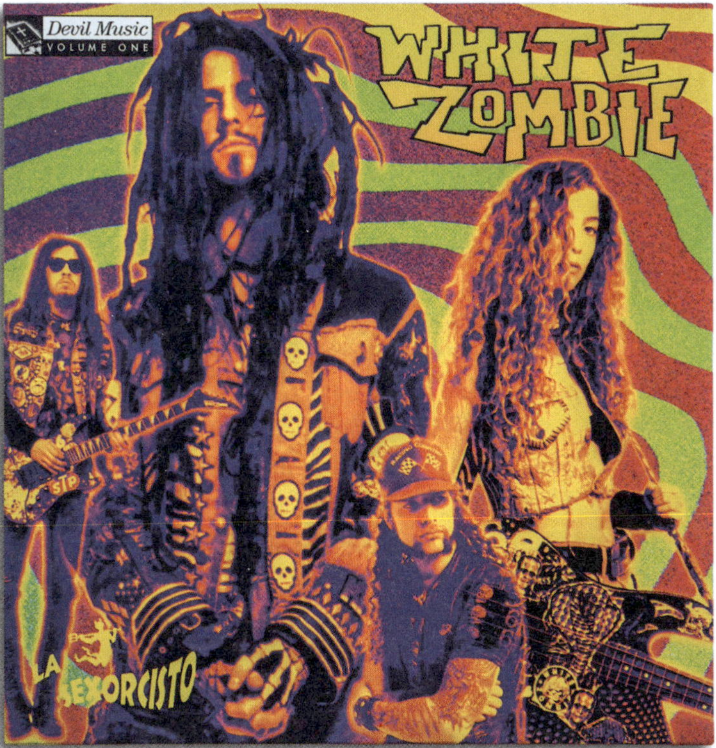

**White Zombie**
**La Sexorcisto: Devil Music Vol. 1**
Geffen Records, 1992
Michael Golob, Rob Zombie, Sean Yseult (Design)
Alison Dyer (Photo)

29 DEC

**Megadeth**
**Countdown To Extinction**
Capitol Records, 1992
Tommy Steele (Design)
Hugh Syme (Illustration)

30 DEC

**Toxic Holocaust**
**Primal Future: 2019**
eOne Music, 2019
Hauntlove (Design)
Steve Chrisp (Illustration)

31 DEC

Imprint

## THE ART OF METAL COVERS VOL. 2

Seltmann Publishers
Berlin, Germany
www.seltmannpublishers.com
info@seltmannpublishers.com

Cover Artworks & Photographs © by the artists

Cover Photos © by Bernd Jonkmanns
www.berndjonkmanns.com

Cover Selection & Background Research:
Christian Kind, Bernd Jonkmanns

Thanks to Chris from Recordstore Plattenkiste for providing his record collection and Johnny Jonkmanns for photo assistance.

Art Direction: Sandro Heindel, Stefan Küstner

We thank everyone involved for their unique artistic work that made this project possible. If you have any questions or suggestions, please do not hesitate to contact us personally.

This project is an homage to the great and glorious decade of vinyl records and their wonderfully designed covers. With this project, we aim to showcase and preserve the covers as well as their high level of artistic power and profound meaningfulness. Every cover has been selected from personal vinyl collections and individually photographed.

Please note:
Not all bands present themselves on Spotify,
so there are various albums without a code.

© 2022 Seltmann Publishers

**ISBN 978-3-949070-24-2**